Wild Apples:

Stories From the Motherline

by

Patricia Celley Groth

cover by Bobbie Groth

photos by Coleen Marks

Patricia Celley Groth

Palanquin Press
University of South Carolina
Aiken, South Carolina

Published by PALANQUIN PRESS
Department of English
University of South Carolina Aiken
471 University Parkway
Aiken, South Carolina 29801

Printed and bound in the United States of America
First printing, 2002
NJ tax exempt #: EA-222-292-741/000

ISBN   1-891508-16-4   (paper)
    1. Title
    2. Women's Studies

Library of Congress Control Number: **2002190700**

by the same author: **Before the Beginning**
                                          The Gods' Eyes

     edited: **Footpath**
                                            Stones and Poets
                                          A Hard Turn

Thanks

I want to thank, first of all, the New Jersey Council on the Arts for two very generous grants that contributed to the creation of *Wild Apples*; Delaware Valley Poets, U S 1, and Stonecoast Poetry Workshop for critiquing these poems, especially Ken Rosen who did it with such humor; William C. Groth for his never ending work on the manuscript; and to Bobbie Groth for doing a wonderful job on the cover. I also want to thank the Geraldine Dodge Foundation for my term as a Dodge Poet; my teachers Herman Ward, Peter Wood, Maxine Kumin, Jane Brown, and Alicia Ostriker, and my colleagues Lois Marie Harrod, Jo Eldredge Carney, Phebe Davidson, and Charlie Groth, for their influence on the poet I have become. Most especially I want thank to my editor, Phebe Davidson, who knew what I had in mind all along — before I did.

I also want to thank some of the women authors who bounded my thought with their thought:

Gene Stratton Porter – " . . . and remember this. What you are lies with you. If you are lazy, and accept your lot, you may live with it. If you are willing to work, you can write your name anywhere you choose; among the only ones who live past the grave in this world are the people who write books that help, make exquisite music, carve statues, paint pictures, and work for others."

Virginia Woolf – "Poetry needs a mother as well as a father."

Elizabeth Coatsworth – "My happiness ran through the centuries/ in one continual brightness…"

Linda Hogan – "Suddenly all my ancestors are behind me. Be still, they say. Watch and listen. You are the result of the love of thousands."

Dedication

This book is dedicated in love to:

my great-grandmothers:
Nellie Ann Tillotson, Margaret O'Heagan Davis,
Adelia Mary Skinner Nute;

my grandmothers:
Mary Bancroft Davis, Katherine Bell Celley;

my mothers:
Helen Elizabeth Celley, Estelle Donnocker Groth,
Marie Golgowski Fick;

my sisters:
Jean Ann Celley, Agnes Groth Klein,
Louise Adelaide Fick Celley;

my cousins:
Dawn Bouton Palmquist, Mary Bouton Briem,
Elizabeth Maud Rumball

and my friends:
Josephine Allegretti Goldberg, Martha Hall Mackenzie,
Roberta S. McIntyre, Joan S. Stewart and Angie Grotheer Dick.

"...death has no country
love has no name."
Mary Oliver

Table of Contents

Preface

The Women in our Family

were not bridge or golf players,
nor were they in love with soap operas—they liked to read.
They all worked, and most of them had families too.
Some had sixth grade educations, DO's, DDS's; some have PhD's,
and DD's, and one worked for Naval Intelligence,
one was a caterer, one made artificial flowers in a factory;
two were medical secretaries, another, secretary for an English Dept.,
one wrote a lonely hearts column for a Boston newspaper.
Some were missionaries, minister's wives; one is a minister,
three were professors, two were grammar school teachers.
We joked about one being an Indian princess, but, in truth,
she was a poor little slave girl captured from the Penobscot tribe
in Maine by a dirty soldier long before the Revolution.
My grandmother told me she married James Nute and was christened
Mary Anne since they didn't know her name. My mother
told me she married Mercy Wentworth Warren's son, which I doubt,
because as far as I can find out, Mercy married James' cousin.
Well, no matter, she married a minister,
and became first in a long line of minister's wives.
The most recent to carry the name is John Warren, minister.
I salute his wife, Ranelle Philomina, beloved queen of his world.

Most were teachers,
many were writers.
But most did not stay home past the time
her youngest child went off to nursery school.
Some did, but they made up for it by being very active
in gardening, canning and freezing fruit and vegetables,
leading Girl Scout troops, PTA's, and Ladies Aid's.
For the most part, they were buxom women,
who knew when to snatch a wedding ring —
and when to leave it alone. Well, some of them did.
Some made disastrous marriages,
but pulled themselves out of a tough spot, thank you.

Lucy married a minister and had never a moment's peace
out there on the Kansas border. He was an Abolitionist.
Fredricka married a von Morstein and left him soon after,
fled to America to do missionary work

in the German ghettoes of New York.

Alma, Wanda, and Geneva, granddaughters,
the "Philadelphia Girls", all had special talents
and took care of themselves until they
were very old women, indeed.
Mary Bancroft was a graduate of the Harvard
Women's Program before it became Radcliffe.

The next generation, Helen, Margery, Stella, Della,
Bertha, and Dora, all lived into their eighties and nineties.
All had careers; all had families. All were role models
for Agnes, Lou, Pat I and Pat II, Ruth, Dawn, Mary Liz —
one secretary in an English Department,
three teachers, one insurance executive,
one travel agency executive, one nurse.
And the women following after —
Bobbie, Karen, Jean, Lori , Kathy,
Norene, Jenny, Linda, Lynn, Dawn, Charlie,
and all the rest, have gone further afield:
one community minister, one audiologist,
two executives, two nurses, one tekkie,
one instructor, one professor, one paralegal.
And their daughters — who knows what they will do?
Kelley, Eva, Corrie, Erin, Annie, Jenna,
Shannon, Keziah and Adelaide, Lindsey, Lauren,
Emma and Elizabeth, Kate and Rosie,
and some more I haven't named.

Yes, we are all strong, determined women
who have overcome a lot of grief in life,
illnesses, deaths, and deadbeat husbands,
but we did it, not with tears —
we kept the tears in our own hearts —
> *but with laughter.*
> > *We showed the whole world*
> > > > *our laughter.*

Wild
Apples

"A story is like water
that you heat for your bath.

It takes messages between the fire
and your skin. It lets them meet,
and it cleans you!"
Rumi

WILD APPLES

for my daughters, Bobbie and Charlie

Some random splice of genes
draws the template for the sweep of brow,
brings the dark color from Black Forest ancestors
for their eyes, shapes them like Indian bows,
blesses them with the long strong bones
of tenth century Danish raiders,
gives them waving chestnut hair,
and a laughing sense of disjoint
to meet this muddled world.

And some power in the cells
gives them the strength
of running water wearing away rock,
the patience of an Egyptian weaver
shuttling ninety yards of white linen,
the courage to plant gardens
and raise children in desert places.

A cord of chromosomes working mindless
in the dark sweet womb,
grants them all Eve's beauty, and Lilith's too,
their need to stay on the outside of walls,
their tug toward wild apples,
red and pungent
        on the tongue.

THE FIRST MARY

I am looking for you, Grandmother, in old cemeteries,
Unitarian, since you married a Unitarian minister,
or maybe even Quaker, since the Quakers
kept an eye out for miserable little Indian girls, like you.
I am looking for signs of you in Town Hall Records,
Church Records, some trace of you written
in some old Bible between soft covers,
the ink softened with time to lavender,
but I don't see you anywhere.

I am looking for you, Grandmother, in the forest,
but only the breeze answers me
with soft sighs like a contented baby;
I am looking over stone walls where birches lean
        into the moonlight, waving;
looking through sunlit meadows
sentried with staffs of goldenrod
and Queen Ann's Lace,
and not finding a trace of you anywhere.

I shall have to look in the folds of my own brain
for memories of you, passed down
from mother to daughter for two centuries.
The first Mary, my grandmother said,
*we never did know her real name
and she wouldn't tell anybody.*

I remember some of the Marys:
there was Mary Maria Nute, Mary Mercy Warren
Mary Skinner Nute, Mary Elizabeth Bancroft;
my grandmother, Mary Bancroft Davis,
and the last Mary, my cousin, Mary Elizabeth Bouton.
No new Mary's in the last two generations.

The earth whispers above all the Mary's, save one,
        keeping their secrets rustling in the grass,
            floating, like Autumn leaves, on the wind.

REMEMBER THE WIND

Sometimes I go about pitying myself,
and all the time I am being carried
on great winds across the sky.
                                    Ojibway

Marie was James's wife.
He bought her in long ago Scituate
from a wandering soldier,
a poor bedraggled Penobscot girl,
couldn't have been more than thirteen,
but hard used, hard used.

I am Little Gray Fox,
the silky one, the sly one.
I have gone behind my face;
you will never find me here.

James's mother looked at the girl, sighed:

Well, if that's what your heart
leads you to, James, so be it. Look
at her face, might as well be
carved out of stone, but she's there.
She's there somewhere.
I'll take her home and scrub her up.

Little Gray Fox went to the river to bathe
and washed her hair until it was shiny.
She dried it in the sun and wrapped it
across her just-beginning-to-grow breasts.
James's mother dressed her in something white,
and walked her back into the river
where an old man invoked the name of God

and said her name would be Mary—
no, Marie, for she had a French look
about her, he said.

She understood the language quickly,
so much simpler than her own,
but said not a word about her mother, father,
little sisters and brothers.
Soon enough she and James
stood before the old man
and James promised:

> *I, James, take thee, Marie,*
> *to be my wedded wife...*

James was kind to her —
she never tried to run away —
but never spoke to him either,
only sometimes she would hum
an Indian lullabye to her babies.
Oo-oo Oo-oo Oo-oo
But there were days
when she would look into the woods,
hear her mother's voice instructing her
from the swirling brown leaves:

> *Remember the sky, Little Gray Fox,*
> *remember the wind.*

MY IRISH GREAT-GRANDMOTHER, MARGARET O'HEAGEN

came from Ireland in 1871 by herself.
She was fourteen years old,
inquisitive blue eyes, wisps of ginger hair
peeking out from her head shawl.
No mother, no father —
both dead in winter's cold.
A brother put her on the boat,
paid her way. She was lucky,
she thought, to find a position
when she stepped off the boat.

"She looks biddable," said the black-skirted nanny
to herself, and took her home to the headmaster.
Out loud she said, *"You'll be working in the house,
not the dorms. You'll be safer there.
An upstairs, upstairs maid,
my sweetie, attic bedrooms."*

She found herself in the employ
of a Boy's Latin School
somewhere outside of Boston.
And there was a boy, Al,
the son of the headmaster and his wife,
who came to the haunt the attic rooms.

They were banished to a Colorado mining town
where his father was half-owner of a silver mine. Al died
of typhus halfway though her pregnancy.
The wife of the other owner of the mine
took care of her until the baby came.

"Such a wee little boy, " Margaret whispered;
  "you'll take him won't you?"

She died three days after the baby was born,
sixteen years old, an ocean and a continent away
from any family that was left to her.
The wife took the baby and baptized him,
Alfred, after his father, *Warren,* after his grandfather.
She took care of him for the next eleven months,
delivered him home to Boston — where his grandmother
would have nothing to do with him.

The Grandfather — what else could he do? —
gave him to some Everett cousins,
who kept him fed, clothed and petted
until he was old enough to go to the Latin school.
He was bright enough, but mischievous,
aiming all his mischief at his Grandfather.
He lived in the dorms, where he had plenty of opportunity
to go drinking and carousing, became quite the ladies' man.

Once he told me that his grandmother
never spoke to him, not even once.
He said,
          "I wonder —
                    what my mother was like?"

THE BURDEN

I am Mary — O there are Marys a-plenty,
(though I am Mara, bitter) I shall be Mary-myrhh;
H. D. *The Flowering of the Rod*

They were coming from Lawrence, Kansas
to Lawrence, Massachusetts on a puffing, blowing train,
and maybe it was because they hadn't reached Presque
    Isle yet
with its surrounding Erie waters, smooth and cool to
    bathe in —
maybe that would've brought the fever down.
Instead they had only reached Cleveland
with its back to the pounding waves,
a crescent white beach separating everything.

My sister died on the tip of morning
in a breathless room squirreled away
in an old boarding house.
Father left to go and make arrangements,
a tiny coffin with a brass plate that said:

Mary Bancroft Nute
August 31st, 1873 — August 31st, 1875

While Father was gone, Mother went into labor.
It went quickly and before he came back, I was born,
a little skinny red girl-child. Father said I should be named
the same name as the little sister who died
because she was named for his mother and his grandmother.
There would always be a Mary Bancroft, he said.

My mother died when I was four
and that's when she, the other Mary,
began to take over my life.

Sometimes she would hit my brother,
or swear, or interrupt Father's sermons
and I would get the blame for it.

It was <u>she</u> who was sent to Switzerland
to the high-priced girls' school
so they could teach <u>her</u> how to behave,
but I had to go along.

She ruined my marriage,
made me leave my children
in a home in Spring Valley,
stood between me and my children
all their lives. People used to laugh at me,
call me Crazy Mary,
but I swear it was really her.

It was hard to do —
        I had to live for both of us.

GREAT-AUNT TILLY

The scent of May came through the open window
of the schoolhouse and tickled Mary Bancroft's nose.
Following the Mayflowers and apple blossoms
she ran out into morning air, not forgetting her lunch.
She ran until she caught up to some 8-year-olds,
Ned and Ted, and Charlie, who had the same idea:
what are we doing shut up in this old schoolroom
when the whole earth smells so sweet?

Arching their backs they skipped and gamboled
like the new little lambs on the next farm over;
they shared Mary's lunch, two boiled eggs, two pieces
of bread-and-butter, a pint can of warm milk,
and a big piece of chocolate cake. They felt so good.
They flew like butterflies down to the little beach
on the brook — really the Concord River, but still a brook
where they were. They took off their shoes and waded
in the water catching hellgrammites and water bugs
skimming on the top making little dimples with their feet.

There came a little chill in the air and suddenly they realized
how wet and bedraggled they were. Silently
they dried their feet on the grass, put on their shoes,
and started back to town. It was a long way through the fields
but eventually they reached the road and Aunt Tilly's house.
Some more fun. Aunt Tilly, Mary's father's aunt,
was as deaf as a crowbar and blind as a mole.
The children crowded behind the lilacs at the side door
and looked through the doorpanes into the kitchen.
Aunt Tilly was ironing. She had an old wood burning stove
stoked to the gills with apple wood, and on top were heating

a heavy old flatiron and heavier old tea kettle.
The children were pointing and giggling
and making big eyes at each other when she did it:
put down the iron to straighten a sleeve,
picked up the teakettle — and ironed the shirt.

They shrieked with laughter, fell down
on the ground and rolled around in a delirium of joy,
never noticing the horse and carriage at the gate.
It was Mary's father, minister of the Unitarian Church,
watching them with a face like a thunderstorm.

With his sermon voice he said, *You Boys, Skeedadle.*
You Mary, walk behind me!
Mary walked down the road
behind the carriage, past the porches
with all the people turned out to see her
in her torn and muddy dress, her dirty face,
her wet hair ribbon hanging down her back.
She felt people's eyes boring into her,
and in return she lifted her chin even higher.

When she was all cleaned up, in her nightie,
and put to bed with no supper, her father came to see her.
You know what you have to do, don't you?
She nodded. *We'll go tomorrow.*
Mary walked down the dusty road behind her father
to Great-Aunt Tilly's little house.
If her father had hoped to teach her a lesson,
it was wrong house to go to. Mary said she was sorry,
but Aunt Tilly didn't hear her, just smiled and said:
God bless the little lamb — coming to see me
so early in the morning. Well, she shall have doughnuts for
her lunch — just made this morning.

Following the corn rows to the schoolhouse, her father said
through stiff lips, *Throw those doughnuts away, Mary.*
God knows what she's put in them.
Ned and Ted were coming from the east, their mother
sailing along the corn like a boat, dragging them by their
    ears;
Charlie was hurrying from the west, but not fast enough
to keep ahead of his father's boot.

Miss Wilton met them at the door, dimples gone from her
    face.
The upshot was they couldn't have recess for a month;
they had sit in the four corners of the room
where they couldn't talk to each other,
and they had to write a hundred times,
I will never run away from school again.

Still she didn't learn the lesson.
Eyebrows drawn over dark, sullen eyes,
Mary promised herself:
    Some day I will get even with you, Father.

And she did, she really did. She became just like him.

THANKSGIVING, 1892

Mary Bancroft, daughter of Rev. Ephraim Nute, is speaking:

The rain was coming down in sheets, it was cold and dark
this night before Thanksgiving, and I stood on the platform,
shivering, and tired from a long semester's work at Harvard.
It was my first time home. I was seventeen.

A cab drew up and I raced to throw my bags
to the coachman, open the door, and throw myself
into the seat. It was after the cab was on its jolting way
that I realized there was someone else in the seat beside me.

It was when I comprehended the white teeth smiling at me
were in a black face, I was overcome with fear and fury.
My knocking almost shattered the isinglass window;
the driver reluctantly let me out along the side of the road.

He said, "You sure you know what you're doing, Miss?"
I didn't answer him, because my head was all full of stories
I had heard from my girlfriends, all about black men raping,
torturing, and murdering – little white girls.

I felt lucky, and brave and courageous to be out of his clutches.
But the longer I tramped along, the more my bravery sank down
into my wet shoes and disappeared into the cold, ankle deep mud.
What if Maisie and Ann weren't right, and what if my father was?

With the wind hurtling at me with such malice, the walk
seemed even longer; the cab came back just in time for me
to catch a glimpse of the black man grinning and tipping his hat.
I had intended to offend him, and he was laughing at me!

Furious again, I ran for home, clattered across the porch floor,

wrenched the glass doors open, and entered the hall,
stood in a big puddle, and shouted, "Father! Father!
I'm home! " He didn't come immediately.

When he did come, his face told me he wasn't happy with me.
I launched into my tale of woe, and he held his hand to stop me.
"Mary, I realize it was long before you were born, but what
    did you
think I was doing all those years in Kansas Territory?"

"Mary, I was not only a minister," he said sternly,
"I was an abolitionist. I kept an underground railway station
in my house, I rode with John Brown, I risked my life for the
    sake
of all Negroes – just like the man you insulted today."

"But," I said, " the stories – don't you believe the stories?"
He said, "The stories that are more likely to be true
are the hangings of poor innocent black men and boys
unjustly accused by ignorant and barbaric women!"

I shrank into myself – yes, there were two sides to every
    question.
"But, Father, " I rallied, "He laughed at me."
"Daughter, " he answered, "we both laughed at you."
My eyes were bright with unshed tears.

"You missed the chance of meeting a young fellow
who might be the most important Negro man of the nineteenth
    century,
most certainly, the twentieth century." Father shook his head —
"and he was coming to ask advice from an old coot like me—
    William Edward Burghardt Dubois."

KISS ME GOODNIGHT

It was the morning of my life, my grandmother said,
thumping her old lady shoes with the heavy heels together,
and since I didn't know <u>it</u> was going to happen,
the sun clouded over that day and never quite came back.

After dishes and prayers I ran down the long meadow
and sat under my own chestnut tree,
cupped my queasy stomach in my hands
and rubbed squashed pennyroyal on my aching temples.
I thought I needed the outhouse and I went to the meadow's
     trinity
of bush and tree and wall where I discovered my woman's
     baptism.
I was so scared I waded into the brook trying to stop
the accusing blood that flowed from my own secret spring.
Finally, when it would not stop, I crept home
and told my step-mother. She laughed at my despair,
said, Mary, this means you have to be careful now —
this is the way babies come.

What way? I said, but she pursed her lips and slapped me hard
in the Old World way. I cried and she said I was difficult;
she would tell my father when he came home from Boston.
They sent me to a girls' school, a stone-walled convent in
     Switzerland,
and though I came back at seventeen, I never felt at home again.
I went to college, married a handsome lad
I met there, bore three children,
and that was noon-time, lunch, Sunday dinner.

In twilight he left me for a girl named Lily
who wasn't even becoming, and I gave the children away.

I was pretty foxy — I put them where <u>he</u> couldn't find them
for two whole years. Afterwards, I was sorry I did that.
When he found them, he parceled them out
to different places. Couldn't be bothered with them,
not with Lily's little boy. Better they had stayed
in the orphanage where at least they were together.

I fled to Europe for ten years and when I came back
my children were snappish strangers,
*   and the long night began.*
I tried everything to get the sun back,
men and booze — and — other things, but why
am I telling you this? Get me a match, will you,
*   Sweetheart?*
There's a good girl — kiss Grandma good-night.

ZERO

When you multiply any number by zero, the end product
is always zero.

1. Grandma's Story

My grandmother told me one quarter of the story —
how she struggled with an alcoholic husband
who abandoned them when was she pregnant,
never paid the rent,
threw their furniture out in the street;
how she single handed rescued her three children
by "trodding the boards," she said,
as a Shakespearean actress on the New York stage,
how she, when she heard he wanted them back,
put them in the place he would never find them —
and he didn't for two or three years. By then, however,
she was out of the country working the immigrant ships
for the government to find where the drugs were coming from.
She said her proudest moment was when she reported to the
        purser
where the drugs were hidden — false bottoms on baby bottles.
She was gone ten years.

2. Mother's Story About Living With Grandma

My mother provided the other three-fourths of the equation.
Ha, when I came home from school I caught her kissing
some other man. She swore it was John Barrymore
and they were rehearsing a part in a play. I didn't believe her.
My father swore the baby wasn't his, and I believed that.
We spent three days and nights on a park bench in Central
        Park.

The baby was born too soon, too frail and died. Her name
  was Miriam.
While all that was going on, my Uncle Frank, eight,
my mother, Helen, six, and my Aunt Margery, four,
were staying in a tent with the Hasselmeyers,
friends of their father's. It was the happiest summer
  of their childhood.

3. Time with Laurette Taylor, Long Gone Actress

Next they moved in with Laurette Taylor,
who had two children, and whose husband
  was also a cipher.
Grandmother had illusions of sharing the stage with her,
but was, instead, baby sitter to all five children.
For money, Grandma had to swallow her pride
and ask my grandfather if he had work for her.
He did — as the Gypsy Lady telling fortunes
on the Boardwalk at Coney Island.
He put Frankie to work selling tickets, and the two girls
singing and dancing as the "Tish Sisters." My mother said,
they always liked Margie better than me.
She was so cute, and what a voice! I was so happy
when I put on my costume — the pink silk, the ruffles —
and so sad when I had to take it off.

4. Poor Old Buddy

There are three things I remember about living
in Miss Taylor's third floor walkup apartment — other
than we hardly ever went to school. The first
was when Margie threw their kitten down the stairwell
to see if it would land on its feet. It did — but never
walked too well after that. Second, was when Frankie

taught me to swim. He tied a rope around my waist
and threw me into the East River.
He didn't know about tides,
so when the rush of water swept me under the dock
against the pilings, well, we both thought I was a dead dog.
A sailor dived in and rescued me. He held me close
all the way up the ladder. I wanted to believe
he was my father, and snuggled even closer.
And the third thing really was a dead dog.
Laurette had a black retriever named Buddy.
One day all five of us took Buddy to the roof, six stories up.
At first we kept him away from the edge of the roof,
but as our excitement escalated, and the dog's did too,
we began to run as fast as we could, the dog after us.
We stopped at the edge,
but Buddy sailed right over the parapet —
down   down   down   to 52nd Street.

5. Spring Valley

We spent another night in the park, because of the dog.
Then my mother took us, bags and suitcases and all,
on the ferry across New York Harbor where we met a train
going to Congers. She hired a horse and carriage
which took us to a big white house with a turret
just outside of Spring Valley. She said we were on vacation,
but overnight she disappeared. It was an orphanage.
Whenever I could, I would go up in the turret and watch
for her.
She never came back. Margie forgot her,
but Frankie and I —
our love turned to bewilderment, then anger, finally — hate.
We were there for two or three years. I forget. Each day
was so like the others. But they fed and clothed us — better

than we had been in years. And they sent us to school —
and soon we were all at the top of our classes.
I thought if I worked very hard and got all A's,
my mother or my father would come back
*   and take us home.*

6. *Father Comes to the Orphanage*

And one evening just at dusk I thought I saw my father
coming up the brick sidewalk, but by the time I scrabbled
*   down from my turret window, he was gone —*
*   taking Margie with him.*
Two days later he came back for Frankie. He took him
during recess. I was shivering inside
*   but never let my lips quiver.*
Finally, he came for me, but he would not meet my eyes.
The Matron had my things packed. It wasn't a little girl
sitting beside him in the carriage — it was a stick of wood.
He explained and explained and explained, but nothing
he said could touch me. I didn't care about his new wife —
what happened to his old one? I never heard anything
*   about a divorce.*
I didn't care about his new little boy. What had happened
to Margie and Frankie? The same old story,
*   but in reverse —*
putting the children where she couldn't find them?
He told me Margie was with a Kingsley cousin,
and my beloved Frankie, had been sent to a boarding school.
He took me home to his apartment in New York — but I
wasn't to stay there. Maudie would be picking me up
in the morning. Who was Maudie?
*   And where was I going?*

I didn't talk to anybody in that apartment — not to Lily,

his new wife, not even to my little half-brother Rob. What
    was the use?
They weren't my family — I had a family of my own
and my father had destroyed it. I lay awake all night
letting my hate for my father grow even larger
than my hate for my mother. She had abandoned us once,
but he abandoned us twice. I could never forgive him.
How could they do that to us? They both had went to college.
Didn't they learn anything?

7. The Catersons

Cousin Maudie came by in the morning — "cousin"
    by some convoluted relationship I never understood,
        but the whole thing turned out lucky for me.
She took me home to her mother and stepfather in Kensico
where I found my real family — a mother who acted
like a mother; a father, gruff, but loving.
Bill and Maud were older than I, in their late teens;
Ed and Grace were younger, practically babies.
I learned how to cook and sew, to ride a horse, to go
    down to New York
by myself and bargain for flowers to use in the business. They
got me a dog, Skippy; they got me clothes like
    Grace's and Maudie's,
even a china doll. Of course — I didn't know my father
paid for everything, paid my board
    all the years I was there.

The only thing they didn't get me was an education. I had
dreams of being a teacher. Instead I worked baby
    sitting Ed and Grace
and in their florist shop to pay my board, I thought.
My mother finally came back, persuaded Margie to go

and live with her in a miserable Brooklyn apartment.
That's when I found out she never did grant my father a
    divorce,
and that's why he didn't want to take us home to his
    new "wife."
My mother couldn't fool me, though; by that time
I had a love of my own — another half orphan, Myrle,
who had grown up in a boarding school until
he ran away and ended up living with the Catersons too.

They were very good to us — but growing up,
    I always felt
I was the one who never got taken care of, the one who
    cared for everybody else, the one who had to fight
    for everything she got.
I always felt I was the mother — and my mother was
    the child.
I was the middle child in whatever home I lived in —
always feeling I was the naught —
                        I was the zero.

WHERE'S THE BABY?

On the verandah, Helen called from the kitchen
on this first day of June in 1924.

No, she's not, he answered.

I left her in the bassinet; her voice was impatient.

She fumbled with the screen door latch.
The lacy mosquito netting was placed with care
around the hood, but the baby was certainly gone.

She stumbled out on the porch. *I left her
right there, not ten minutes ago.*
Stunned at this second loss — the first baby gone
before it had even lived and the doctors
had told her she would never have another one.

All through the Vermont hospital days with skies like granite
she had turned her heart to what she could have —
a baby from foster care — this baby.
Hoping to adopt her, they gave her a new name:
Sandy. Certainly better than Edna.

They kissed her over and over, saw her first smile,
walked the floor with her in the night,
until they thought surely she must be theirs.
They thought her mother would never
come out of Grasslands Reformatory.

And now this — this note on the pillow:
I come for what's rightfully mine.
Thank you for taking such good care of Edna.
I will return the clothes when I get on my feet again.

The police just shrugged their shoulders, said: *she's right:*
you don't have any blood or legal ties to that baby.

The clothes came back a long time later
showing signs of much wear.

Stone faced,
Helen buried them in the garden.

OUT OF THE STARS

Out of the stars, she came, my sister,
born during a Twilight Birth,
which was supposed save the mother
from feeling any pain, but instead
left damaged babies in its wake —
  the ultimate, shuddering pain.

They never knew what visions
her crossed eyes were delivering
to her head; she scarcely talked, she
couldn't run, she wet her bed.
The doctor said, *Put her in an institution — she'll
never be any better than she is right now.*

In their defense, my mother
had a terrible kidney infection
in that time of no antibiotics,
they were expecting a new baby
and they had two toddler boys.

They walked up the brick walk, her little palms
pressed against theirs. *She trusted us, don't you see,
she trusted us.* Every brick in that huge building
felt like a wheelbarrow full of bricks on their hearts.

Going home in their old Model A,
my mother weeping beside him, my father
ran red lights, went left where he should've gone right,
went sporadically fast and slow, all because
he couldn't see past the blur in his own eyes.

They left her there for two days. The joy in living drained
  out of them. The little boys asked, *Where Jeannie go?*
and they didn't have any answer for them.

And then Aunty Ann came in the door like a whirlwind,
said, *I've just seen Jeanie! You've got to get her out
of that place. She is sitting on the floor,
rocking back and forth, whimpering, hiding
her head in her arms — I'll mind the boys.*

They left immediately, left the frying pan on the stove,
left the baby sitting in his high chair.
When they came home, she was buttoned
against my father's chest. She was so cold,
so cold.

When they were going through the hallway
hurrying my sister along, a woman, a matron,
came running after them yelling, *You can't have her! She's
a ward of the state now — you signed these papers!*
She waved a sheaf of papers at them.

Inspired, my mother turned to meet her,
grabbed the papers, and tore them into little shreds.
There, said my mother, *you can't prove
she was ever here. And don't you follow us!*
My mother must have looked menacing
because no one followed them, and when they
got home, they called a lawyer.

That lawyer must have had some clout, because
nobody from the home or state ever came after them.
I heard he was legal counsel for Lithuania, Latvia,
and Estonia. Oddly enough, his name was Mister Law.

My mother took care of her for all of her thirty-three years,
persuaded the principal of the local school to let her go to
    "school"
with her brother, sat with her during measles, mumps, tonsils,
diabetic comas and with all being diabetic means. She even

took a job in the city hospital so she could stay
 near my sister
in the last months. We all took turns staying with her —
brothers, sister, cousins — until the end came.

On the last day of her life, she stirred a little,
 opened her eyes.
My mother and cousin Bess were there holding her hands.
She whispered, *Mama, can I go now?*

My mother said, *Of course, dear. You can go now.*
And while they held her hands, she passed
back to the stars where she came from.

SOMETHING TO CRY ABOUT

My brothers and sister
are caught in a cup of gold
lighting the hairs of their heads
in exquisite Renaissance chasing
as they turn around, expectant faces
away from the western sun
and toward the gas stove
where our mother is cooking dinner.
Sunlight floats through
the bank of windows
and reveals a rich life
in the green and cream squares
of the linoleum.
The cat, striped and white vested,
dangerous with his needled feet,
sits on the corner of the table
watching the sputtering pan,
the black tip of his tail twitching,
the pink tip of his tongue
caught between his teeth,
catching the smell of frying bacon.

Hiding behind the swinging door,
my fourth-hand Dr. Dentons
drooping and washed-out gray,
I stretch my baby hand high, higher
toward the shiny, blue-ringed bowl
on the Hoosier cabinet.
It is full of eggs,
brown and delectably smooth,
gorgeously shaped, heavy with promise.
Higher, higher.

I get one, hold its perfection
for a moment before it slips,
as it must, through my fingers,
splats on the floor.
The sound is delicious.
Fascinated, I watch
the great yellow eye
spread out from the shattered shell.
My brothers wail
in a Greek chorus,
Mama, look what the baby did!
My sister says nothing,
keeps her eye on the frying pan,
the bubbling pots.
The cat has disappeared,
the sun gone down.

I start to cry
over the murdered egg,
the ancient knowledge
that punishment will follow.
My mother looms large,
wet cloth in hand,
wipes the egg white spatters
from my feet and legs,
continues over the floor
until the squares come back.
She unlocks her pursed mouth
to call out in exasperation,
Keep quiet, all of you,
or I'll give you something
to cry about!

As if our weeping
wasn't real.

SUNDOWN TOMORROW

I hit death head on, twice, in my sixth year
when we were living on Trenton Avenue.
I went up the steps of the house next door
and knocked on the sun porch door, then opened it.
I knew better than that, but I really wanted the nickel
Miss Polly promised me for bringing her
a loaf of bread from the corner store.
She showed me two nickels, said, *That's for the bread,*
and this other nickel is for you when you come back.

She was sitting in her wicker rocker, head turned like a
    sleeping bird,
mouth open, eyes shut. She looked no different than my
    napping Grandma.
I went around the room looking at things — a little birch
    bark canoe
from Alaska, a marvelously colored *fleur-de-lis* in a glass
    egg,
a nest of Russian dolls. It was taking a long time for her
    to wake up.
All of a sudden my mother was in the room, come
    looking for me.
She shook Miss Polly, said, *Oh my God,* and went
    directly
to the telephone and after that she rustled me out of there.
I protested, *She's only sleeping! And I want my nickel!*

She sent me to my room. How did I know Miss Polly
    was dead?
I watched from my window, watched the doctor pull up
in his rattly black Ford, go in the back sun porch door;
watched the hearse from Ballard's back up to the door,

watched the men take Miss Polly out on a stretcher,
watched them slam the doors on the hearse and drive away.
No more Miss Polly.

When my brothers came home from school, they said
how lucky I was to see a real dead body. They made me
    describe
the way she looked over and over, not realizing
their turn to see a dead body would come soon.
A few weeks later a May storm came up in the West.
We hurried to get into our pyjamas before the lights went
    out.
We scurried down the stairs and sat in the window-seat
waiting for the show to begin. We saw the neighbor
on the other side of our house drive into his driveway
in a sudden burst of rain. We didn't know him;
he came and went so silently. Soon the storm was
    overhead;
we gasped at each bolt of lightning, each peal of thunder.

We saw the lightning hit his car.

Our father said he would have been all right if only
he had grounded the car against the drainpipe
before attempting to get out of it. As soon as he set foot
on the ground, we saw his body outlined in blue.
He fell to the ground and we saw him burst into flames.
Burnt to a crisp, my brother breathed reverently, *burnt to a
    crisp.*
Once again I watched the doctor come; but this time
he came with police cars and ambulance. Once again
I watched them pull open the doors and put the stretcher in.

Is it any wonder I had nightmares? After the third night

of screaming and sobbing, my mother and father
looked wearily at each other,
and in some language unknown to me, they nodded.
Get packed, Helen, my father said.
We'll be out of here by sundown tomorrow.

HOODOO DOLL

Shirley Temple — a miracle under the tree,
her dimples and blonde curls,
dotted swiss dress and real leather slippers
asking to be stroked.
But she was my sister's. Not mine.
Watch her eyes, Mama said.
If they shine, she knows,
or, *if they shine, she loves you back.*

In time we fought over Shirley,
breaking her fingers, her toes,
and my sister, sobbing, gave her to me.

Mama said, *Well, she's yours now, Miss.*
Keep her, and maybe some good will come of this.
The doll stood on my dresser watching me
until the dank of old houses cracked
her glass gaze and I hid her away
where she lived just under
the slack of memory until finally
I had to free her from the black eaves.

In my bedroom, a whole lifetime
since she stood under the spruce,
Shirley poses in her puffy new dress,
sewing machine oil in her blind eyes,
and I talk out loud to her sausage curls:
Remember, Shirley, I say,
Remember when I said I wouldn't,
but I broke you anyhow
and made my sister cry?

Tell me on this present Christmas Day
so far away from wild screams and whining,
you forgive that possessed child,
darker than any little movie Satan,
who wanted you with such passion
and then never played with you again.
Sweet Shirley, Little Miss Marker —
    yes, it's true — your eyes are shining.

THE SNOW TROLLS

Something startles me awake;
I peek across the snow-humped bushes
looking like evil trolls
that are coming to get me.
At last I fall asleep again.

In the morning the sour smell of frying eggs
tells me again my stomach hates eggs.
I run for the warm kitchen and a millisecond
before my foot touches the hot air register,
I hear the roar of burning coal beneath.
Screaming, I throw myself into the one empty chair.
My brothers and sister are already there;
I am always the late one.
I land on the cat who rakes my thigh.
My father calls for iodine, white socks, butter.
He does not say *Why are your slippers in your hand?*
but quirks his eyebrow which means the same thing.

Where is Mommy? I ask,
finally noticing her ponderous bulk
is not filling the kitchen.
Mommy's sick, but she's alright, my father says.
Eat your breakfast and get ready for school.

I cannot eat and at school there is only the teacher,
and six walkers and a limper — me.
I have no milk money
and when I open my lunch bag,
it is a fried egg sandwich.
I think I must have gotten some other kid's lunch,
but I swallow my crying and throw my lunch away.

In Reading Group I call the teacher *Mommy* by mistake
and the other children laugh.
I bite my cheeks for the taste of blood;
my foot throbs; my cat scratch stings.
Walking home I expect Mommy will be there,
but a neighbor lady opens the door.

I decide my mother is dead.

Every day there is a different lady;
and I do not believe her when she says to send notes
and drawings to the hospital like my brothers do.
I know my mother is dead.

I never eat breakfast and I throw my egg lunches away
until one day I gather courage
and offer to make my own lunch.
My foot heals, the clumsy peanut butter sandwiches
keep me from starving,
and the tears calcify into a gravestone in my chest.
I am proud of myself —
I have never once let them out through my eyes.

One day I plod through the snow,
and my mother is lying on the couch.
She holds out her thin arms, but I will not run to her.
I want to scream at her, hit her, butt my head into her
      stomach.
All that pain and fear, that fried egg and peanut butter —
all for nothing?
I run for the bathroom,
vomit up the hard ball of swallowed tears and sobs.
When I come out, I am trembling, but I go to her,
bring her all my school papers, drawings, and poems,

sit beside her like a Spring frog,
drawing sunshine from her approval.

Not until twenty years later do I tell her
about Daddy's fried egg lunches and the time
I thought she was dead.
Then she tells me what I never knew before.
That night I woke to snow trolls,
after we were all in bed,
she had washed out our clothes,
but when she went coatless to hang them out,
her foot slid on a piece of ice
and her swollen body pitched down the back stairs.
Helpless, blacking in and out from cold and pain, she felt
her baby's water pillow draining through her dress,
freezing on her legs, until my father came home
from stoking his greenhouse fires.
An hour later in the hospital she gave birth to twin boys.
Three months early, they didn't have a chance.

Listening to her story, I felt a chill
chatter deep in my womb —
the snow trolls got us after all, got our babies,
only as big as Christmas didee dolls,
my tiny brothers I never knew.

My mother, forty-one years old,
got pneumonia and phlebitis;
in that day of no magic medicine,
I had not been too far wrong
in believing her dead all those frightful weeks.
But you know, she said, *your father never asked
"why did you do such a foolish thing,*

go out there on the back porch on the coldest winter's
        night?
I would have hung the clothes for you."
I knew all that, my mother said,
and I was grateful he never put it into words.

But, I answer, *he quirked his eyebrow so — right?*
And we contemplated together the quiet, gentle man
who must have despaired, but never held us accountable
for our thoughtless deeds,
let us say —
the snow trolls came.

MUD PUDDLE

It was, my mother said,
rainbow light in our front yard,
a pale iridescence
reflected in a huge puddle
between summer storms
that August of my eighth year.
The rainbow was behind us,
behind the house and hill
where we could not see it,
but its reflection was enough
and we stripped to our cotton panties,
my sister, my brothers and I,
and we jumped straight off the porch
into the ankle deep water
sending sprays of shimmering dots
into the pearly air.
We jumped and pushed
and smacked the water upward
with the palms of our hands.
My sister gave up first
and retreated to the old bedspread
Mother was holding up on the porch
to catch our mud and water.
My older brother went next,
shivering and asking for hot chocolate.
My younger brother and I
duked it out in the thick gloppy mud,
but I finally sent him scrambling,
blinking the brown water
from his blue eyes, and protesting
my savage attack. *That's no fun,* he said,

stamping up the porch steps
to the bedraggled bedspread.

Now it was mine, this mud puddle
churned into brown cake batter.
I laid down in it, my arms and legs
stretched wide, and then together,
wide and together. And it held me there;
the earth held me in its grip
as if I were nothing more than a stone
rolling around in eternity.
I could not move my limbs.
Terrified, I knew I was sinking
and soon the slithery mud
would enter my eyes and nose and mouth.
I would be dead in the rainbow light.

Just then my mother called my name
and released the spell. I freed myself
from the muddy mortar and stood up
very carefully, not disturbing even one inch
of the wings and gown printed in our front yard.

How nice, my mother said, *a mud angel.*

TEA PARTY

It was a little soft pink granite house
I happened on by accident one day
when I was nine years old, old enough
to know what cemeteries were for,
but young enough to follow a small gravel path
in the hopes of finding something delicious,
something like a gingerbread house
without an old witch being around to spoil
my exploring for gold and tootsie rolls.

And there it was, the shade of pink cotton candy,
and set on the tiny porch between the fluted columns
were two baskets of pansies with their little faces
looking at me, daring me to come
and try the grill-work door.
It was open, of course, on this faerie-tale day
in late August, open — and I walked in.

Inside, much to my wonderment,
there was a lamb traced on the floor
in gold, green, blue. I soon realized
it was the sunlight coming through
a stained glass window in the back wall,
a sort of Gemini of lambs.

There was a long drawer on the side of the room,
and in back under the window
there was a little table and chairs.
I set up shop as quickly as I could,
sneaking my tea set and two favorite dolls,
Nancy and Betsy-Wetsy, into the little house.
I played for hours never giving a thought

to the inscription on the drawer:

Miriam Grace   1910-1919
May this Lamb of God rest in peace.

But finally my father found me,
said the people who owned the mausoleum
wouldn't like my playing there —

so close to their little girl.

THE KING AND QUEEN OF BLACKBERRYING
FEED THEIR ROYAL CHILDREN

My father was a methodical man.
The big blackberry patch on the hill
just below the rocks and above the sand pit
had the largest, blackest, best berries in Valhalla —
and fairly free of Japanese Beetles too.
One Sunday in the heat, he put on his work shirt,
pulled on a pair of thin leather driving gloves
and started clipping out trails among the thorns.
First, he determined his reach, so little paths
would not be too far apart for his range.
He took his clippers, and top to bottom,
pruned the spiny briars, raking them into heaps
at the bottom of the hill. He had a pot
all ready so it hung down from a harness
on his neck. He picked the berries
from the cut branches, enough for one day.
He took them home, washed them gently
at the porcelain-covered iron sink.
These were for our supper, purple and sweet.

The next evening after work and supper
he really got down to business pulling
the berries into his pails. He let me walk
with him to the patch. I learned
quick enough not to ask if I could pick too.
"No, Honey," he'd say, *"you'll scratch your arms."*
When he said *"no,"* you learned early not to whine.

Soon the kitchen overflowed with blackberries, pots,
pans, and buckets — and with them came my mother,
after work, after dinner, after dark,
dressed for jelly making in house dress, apron,
socks, slippers, hair net, rubber gloves — no corset.

She kept two colanders going, one for rinsing,
one for picking over the berries. Four gas burners,
four pots — two for cooking the blackberries,
two for boiling jars and lids.
She mashed the berries in the one pot
and put it on the burner to cook.
"Can I help?" I asked. *"No, no, Sweetheart,"*
she answered, *"you'll burn yourself."*
I watched through the hot steam
as she fixed the curtain over the second pot,
poured the cooked blackberries
through the gauze to catch those tiny seeds
that got under her plate
and hurt like the dickens,
and then she hung up the bag to drip.

But one Saturday she needed me.
It was when she tipped up the sugar bag
and saw it was crawling with ants.
"Oh, darn!" she exploded.
"I know!" I said, *"I can ride to the village
on my bike and bring back more sugar!"*
I felt like a gladiator pedaling fiercely
down the macadam parkway path,
up the sidewalk to Cesaeres' Market.
It was a mile each way and I made the whole trip
in less than a half hour. I was proud of myself,
and now I felt I had a part in those rows and rows
of gleaming jars filled with blackberry jelly.

Come winter, we never gave a thought
when we reached for our jelly sandwiches
how hard they worked overtime
in wartime darkness to feed us
              with those garnet jewels of August.

FLICKA

My 10th birthday, after school,
I stood in the cavernous door of the gym, cautious.

She, the green Girl Scout lady shook my hand,
the grimy one, black with pencil lead, and said, *Hi,
I'm Flicka. You're Patty Celley, aren't you?*
Magic. Witchcraft. She swept me up
in a dancing singing game, a funny one where we all
were flapping like geese and singing as loud we could
Why doesn't my goose sing as loud thy goose?

She came along when I was ready to do anything.
Scavenger Hunts with patrols — I learned how
to step up to any door and ask for strange things.
One was a note of apology
    for something you had never done.
The man and lady led the eight of us into their house,
down a corridor, and into a garage with skylights.
I had never been in an art studio before.

Oh, what fun! the lady said,
and they set about making the note:
a skull and crossbones, a map of an island,
an X on the map to show where treasure lay.
The note read: *I'm sorry you wasn't here
to divide the loot, Here's your part.
Signed: The Wicked Ones*
They lit a candle and singed the edges
of the paper. Then they crumpled it all up,
spread it out, and folded it neatly.
There, show this to Flicka, they said laughing,
she'll know where you went.

I was doing a badge in Astronomy
and I had questions for Flicka.
She told me to go to the library,
but the library was closed so I asked my grandmother.
She had a son in the Navy and told me to write the
    director
of the Naval Observatory. I got a two-page letter back
saying he was glad to hear from me.
I held on to that letter for years
but it got thrown out when I went off to college.

She was really Mrs. Fick,
Flicka, filly, a play on names,
a metaphor for everything bright and shining —

   a red horse leading me on
        to wide open blue skies.

TIME TRAVEL

Mrs. Fury, Fifth grade,
I wrote in careful up-and-down script,
and that was my first mistake,
the first of many, for she didn't seem to like
any of the answers I gave
to what I thought were rather personal questions,
 Do you live with your father?
 your mother?
 your grandmother?
even if the answer was *yes.*
And arithmetic — she shamed me before the rest
because I never could do the time test, add
the numbers so fast, find an answer
all nice and neat at the bottom.
You're woolgathering, Patty,
always off in a world of your own,
she would say, her mouth pursed into a hard rosebud,
her eyes hard and white like a statue.

That's when I stopped trying, let go,
and floated out the third-story window,
over the wall, over the trees, the Taconic,
the Bronx River, and the New York Central.
I swam along in the air, keeping the parkway
on my right, the railroad on my left,
the river shining just below me.
I passed Thornwood, Chappaqua, Mt. Kisco,
all the way to Hyde Park and that's
where my imagination failed me, having
been there only once with my father in the Rose Truck
delivering baskets and baskets of flowers.

I waved to Eleanor and Fala,
did a U-turn and started back.
I did this so many times
I was more out of the classroom than in it.
Then one day I vaguely heard a voice saying,
  Hold out your hand.

I received a blow from the business side of a ruler
across the knuckles of my left hand.

I knew if I told them at home, I'd get another crack,
so I stayed in the classroom from then on,
actually learned to do sums and parse sentences.
She stopped asking those nosy questions —
I even learned to spell her name right:
  Mrs. Fiore.

UNDER THE BRIDGE

I

At twelve,
I stood in the clear brook running the dark space
under the bridge, stone-capped like an English keep,
but so tiny and useless here where sleep lay
almost humming outside the secret nook.

Tea strainer in my hand, I could achieve a stillness
my mother would never believe if she too hadn't stood
just so in this water a lifetime ago catching ancestors
to these pollywogs in her mother's Mason jar. There!
Swish! I kidnapped a fat, green alderman
and slid him into my battered pail. He would become
a Chicago mayor back home in my old roasting pan
that served me as a pond.

A door thunked close by this harbor under the bridge
so private in its stipple of umber light, guarded by its fringe
of tiny stalactites. I forgot my chilled bones in the fever
of watching people, more vital, surely, than hellgrammites
                or satin frogs.

II

Genevieve helped her gnarled grandfather
into the grape arbor next to the frothy little race.
She put his deck of cards on the kitchen table charred
by long-gone pots and smoking bread.
She came with a black-eyed child buttoned
to a rubber nipple and plunked him into a playpen
next to the old man, each in his own jail.
Now I heard the three other old men,
stone cutters no longer for sale,

shuffling on the road over my head,
and running calloused hands like files
over the bridge's toothy stones.

I saw them turn under the grape leaves,
eager to start their daily game. Genevieve
brought red wine; the players were all smiles.
Now Grandpa, she said, *You watch Rosario
while I start to cook.*

The old man sent her a look
and continued to pass
the kings and queens among the four —
a long silence and then the bids
rising from marble dust throats.
Rosario, the living image of some angelic carven mute,
waved his fat legs and sucked even more.
The locusts filled the air with their thrumming,
and it seemed this peace was absolute —
until I caught a glance on the old man's face
of such despair and loss,
the golden day shattered, and along with him,
I saw the darkness coming.

III

Even back then, I wanted to shout
and tell this wine-soaked old fellow
everything would be all right,
but I didn't own the courage,
or maybe I already knew it was a lie.
I waded back through the little cave
and just before the yellow slip-slap
of reflected tiny waves, I tipped my bucket out
and watched the almost-frog curl away
    under the bridge.

BACK TO THE SUN

It was in the Church of the Highlands —
the first funeral I ever went to as a genuine mourner.
All my life I had gone with my florist father
to funerals and funeral homes,
an invisible mouse-brown child
skulking around grown-up legs
or waiting silently in the panel truck
with its painted roses, throwing furtive
glances through open back doors
at guttered tables with their naked burdens.
If they hadn't been dead, they soon were,
finished by the mortician's
need to keep his own wolves at bay.
I didn't care; I would have sorrowed
over kittens or puppies or fawns,
but grown-ups I didn't know
moved my child's heart no more
than standing rib roasts.

Our nearest neighbor lived
a quarter of a mile back in the woods,
wise woman, mother of Dormouse,
my favorite dog I took care of a whole year
while she and Sam, her husband,
traveled in Europe and sent back postcards
of Neuschwanstein's dark whiteness,
and Kingsbarns' dry stone walls.
Driver of station wagons (my mother couldn't drive),
a medical doctor (my mother twisted wire stems
in an artificial flower factory),
she took me with her and Sam
to hear Mozart's music, to see O'Neill's plays,

and I learned there were other topics
than money, kids, or politics
a man and wife could talk about.
Older now, one Sunday afternoon,
still dressed in my church clothes,
I gathered my courage to ask her the question,
and quickly walked the path between the trees to her
    house.
We talked of this and that until I finally blurted out,
    What can I do about my skin?
She didn't laugh, bless her, but took my chin
in her cool, thin-fingered hand,
gazed into my face a long time
until my despair made me sorry I had asked.

Finally: *I can give you something
that will help,* she said,
*but more important you should know
you are a pretty girl;
you have beautiful shiny hair;
your eyes have glints of gold,
and you already know how to dress
the young woman you are.
You have too much to give
to let these silly spots stand
between you and the world.*

I have fed on these words
for almost sixty years.

Then she showed me
that in death there is living.
Dying of cancer, she journeyed
one last time across the country
and when she returned,

she whispered, *Lake Michigan, Grand Canyon,*
the Rockies—all part of me. Now I'm ready
to go up in flames, back to the sun.
And so I mourned in that church
as best a girl of fifteen can,
not knowing the thanks I would owe her
for the person I have become.
But when youngsters come desperate
to my office, crying their fatal flaws,
I say, *Come on, we'll work on it; look how well*
you turn that phrase, make that real insight.
You have too much to give to let these little failures
get between you and the world.

And these young men and women
become part of me
as I glance toward the sun;
I become a part of them
as they move past me
      into their own planes.

WATCHING THE BIRDS

My grandmother met me at the back door,
excitement in her black eyes;
she was a doing a little dance
in her old lady black shoes,
clearly glad to see me.

But I was fourteen, grouchy,
all ready to be rude to someone,
and she was it. *So what did
you do all day?* I still
remember the sneer,
the impatience in my voice.

*I was watching the birds.
Oh, you should have seen
the dear little things!
Gold bodies and black wings,
pointing their tiny faces
to look into mine.*

I didn't pay attention to her words,
not then, but a half century later,
they are carved into stone.
Especially when my neighbor's child
comes into the garden
asking the same thoughtless question.

I talk to her retreating back:

*I'm watching the birds,
    just watching the birds.*

THE GIFT

> *You have to care enough about someone to be honest*
> *enough to hurt them – that which hurts, instructs.*
>   *Peter Ralston*

I was my daddy's darling, nevertheless,
when I came home from school whining about something
the teacher, Miss Baloney, as we called her, did or said to me,
he would give a crooked smile under his mustache
and say, *That's character building.*

I was eight years old and finally
got a handle on the multiplication tables.
I stood beside my seat and recited them
expecting Miss Baloney to praise me.
Instead she said, *August, will you see*
if she has all that written on her desk?

I hurt so much I didn't hear what August said,
ignored her backhanded compliment,
and I never told Daddy
about my character building experience.
But I never trusted her again.

I could hardly wait to be promoted out of her class,
but, Gloryosky, when I went to Junior High,
she went with me, as my homeroom teacher,
and later in ninth grade as my algebra teacher.

When she had her back turned to the class
doing something at the blackboard,
I developed a way of imitating her, *sotto voce,*
which had my classmates dissolved in giggles.
She would whirl around — and never catch me,

although her iron eyes looked right through me.

Then one day she filled three boards
with an eighteen step proof. She stepped back,
nodded, as if to say, "can you do better than that?"
I raised my hand. *I can do that in four steps.*

Prove it. Her voice was hard.
It was then I had a premonition,
a chill which I shook off too soon.

I went to the board and wrote quickly
feeling certain I was right.
Turning from the board I caught a glimpse
of an expression on her face; she seemed suddenly —
deflated, her face pale. *But*, she said slowly,
I haven't shown you how to do that yet.
I was suddenly sorry for what I had done to her.
She, however, bided her time until the last day of school.
Birdie and I were fooling around in the empty library,
snatching each other's shoes and flinging them
onto the depleted shelves. Higher and higher.
Swallowing our laughter, I raced to retrieve the shoe
I just had thrown, only to discover
    it was nowhere to be found.
It had fallen into the hole formed by the ends of bookcases
in the corner of the room. It was a long way down.

We looked at each other and said, *Let's go call Mr. Reilly.*
We told him all about our predicament. He laughed
and assured us he would fix it. The last bell rang,
and Birdie had to a hop, skip, and jump
    back to our homeroom,
one shoe on, one shoe down the hole.

Miss Baloney leaped on her, drew the story out of her,
insisted on storming back to the library, two miserable girls
    in tow.

Mr. Reilly handed her shoe to Birdie, but, no,
    Miss Baloney
intercepted it, said, *No, you don't — this girl* (meaning me)
has to learn some discipline. You two sit here and wait.
Our buses left and Birdie was stricken, *what about my
    mother?*
I didn't have anybody waiting at home for me. They all
    worked.

The teachers filed into the library
    for the last teachers' meeting.
Miss Baloney sat at the long table
    with Birdie's shoe in front her.
Birdie sat on her foot to save it
    from the mean glances aimed at it.
Soon they were all at it hammer and tongs,
trying to decide my punishment.
Birdie tried to say, *I threw her shoe too*,
but nobody was listening.
Finally, Miss Baloney rapped on the table with Birdie's shoe,
said, *She's going to high school next fall and she's*
supposed to go into the Scholarship Group. Well, I don't think
she's disciplined enough to succeed there,
so why don't we start her in the Medium Group?
They all murmured what a good idea, and they were gone
for the summer leaving the shoe lonely on the table.

So I started in the Medium Group
with Miss Harvey for an English teacher,
determined to work my way up to Scholarship.

I sat in her room the hour before school started
because it was the only room open so early in the
    morning.
She introduced me to this tall boy with such dark eyes
it was almost like looking into his soul. He had the
    prettiest ears.
Bill was his name and I allowed him to help me
with math and German — and he was in the scholarship
    class.

Next term they moved me to the Superior Group
and into Bill's German class. *Deutschland über alles.*
It has been over fifty years and I still think he has the
    prettiest ears;
his wavy dark hair is gone with the wind, and he has
    grown a curly white beard to balance his nose,
    but oh yes, when I look into his gypsy dark eyes
I still see his soul looking back.

I worked like a dog and at the end of that semester
there was a note in my report card,
You have been promoted to the Scholarship Class.
Senior year. I had scholarships that would pay my way
completely to a little college high in the Catskills.
I was so happy there.

After Christmas I had an errant idea about going to the
    author
of all my worst dreams and settle it with her.
I took a bus to Mt. Kisco, walked to the old Victorian
    house
where she had an upstairs apartment. I rung the bell,
    suddenly hoping against hope
      that there was no one there to answer it.

But there was. She answered the door, drew me into
    the tiny hall,
so happy to see me. I had never seen her smile that
    way before;
I knew if I didn't say soon what I had come there to say,
I wouldn't say it at all. So I blurted out:
Why were you so mean to me?

I watched her face change, grow serious.
Because I loved you. Because I knew you had so much
    potential.
Because I knew your parents would never discipline you; I
had to wake the determination in you to be the best you
    could be.
And I wasn't wrong, was I?

The Righteous Rev. Sue said in a sermon
you must forgive your enemies
and you must thank those, with a smile,
who had so much to do with the person you became.

Today I answer your question, Miss Malone.

No, you weren't wrong. You gave me a great gift
that day in the library, but I was too unaware
to realize it and appreciate it. You gave me determination
and all the gifts that have followed in its wake,
a long and a happy marriage, recovery from operations,
illnesses, and two cardiac arrests, five children
I am very proud of, set on their way in life, three degrees
earned after the birth of my children, a part-time career
as a college professor and an almost PhD,
cut short by a devastating stroke. That

required the most determination of all —
to learn to walk and talk and write again.

I thank you, Miss Malone, not with a smile,
with tears.

DEAR LITTLE SISTER

how are you I am fine
dog is fine cat is fine
I miss you I love you
are you coming home soon
                    love from Jean Ann

All that first September in college
I inhaled mountain air and Emily Dickinson
in great gasps of freedom.
The band coiling my throat loosened
and I sang the songs seventeen sings.
The granite on my shoulders
thinned to dust and blew away
so my pony tail bounced
like any other girl's.

But with killing frost,
they came, the weekly letters,
always the same, from my older sister
who was permanently immured
in the nursery of mind and home.
I could close my eyes
and see her at the dining room table,
clenching a pencil so hard it bends,
staring so hard her eyes cross
and she has to stop and let them go back.
I can smell the ever-present Vicks scarf
wrapped around her throat
covering the scar
she doesn't want anyone to see.

Sometimes the letters of my name
walked across the envelope
and fell off the sides;
other times my mother's
hopscotch hand caught my baby name
and flung it impatiently on the white square.
Either way, I thrust the envelope
deep inside my feedbag purse
and hurried away, hoping nobody saw.

But every moment, every year,
the weight grows heavier
until now, decades later,
I can scarcely lift my feet.

I have carried that purse
a long time.

MARY AND MYRLE

They told her, the grandmother, to stay and watch the house
while they, the mother and her daughter,
went downtown to shop for Easter;
so she watched the jello with sour cream set,
kept an eye on the rising bread dough,
went outside, looked through her opera glasses
at the horses cantering on the side of the hill.
Sighing at the length of afternoon, she went inside,
loosed her long white hair from combs and bun,
laid her tall, skinny body down in her narrow bed,
composed herself for sleep, which would not come.

She was worried about Myrle — her son-in-law.
She loved fixing lunch for him, and usually,
on days when the rest of them were gone,
they would laugh and smoke, tell
some slightly scatological stories.
But this day he didn't talk much, said
he had the monster of all headaches. Another thing,
he took the collie with him, which he never did.
She watched him whistle the dog up onto the seat;
the windows of the truck were open and the dog's ears flying
as they pulled out of yard in a burst of sand and gravel.

She tried to read, couldn't, threw the book down.
(It was *Walden*.)   She said with contempt,
What did David know about anything?
Poor little spoiled Mama's boy!
She crossed her legs, screwed her eyes shut,
and then she heard it, a sort of bump and slide,
Myrle's voice calling, *Mary, Mary, come and help me.*

She raced down the stairs as fast as her poor old bones
would let her; she found him sitting at the kitchen table,
his face ashen and all slid to one side,
trying to take off his boots.

He had walked home with the anxious collie whining
beside him. Mary wanted to call the doctor,
but he wouldn't let her.
Just help me up the stairs.
I want to die in my own bed.

And so they went, one painful step at a time
until they reached the walnut bed
where he sat down. She lifted
his legs into the bed and covered him,
brought a wet cold washcloth for his headache,

watched him die before her very eyes.

PALE HANDS AND MOEBIUS STRIPS

My mother's hands
were like white butterflies flitting
against the greens she was arranging
for some holiday
or special celebration —
a birthday, perhaps,
or an engagement.

Her hands so well-shaped —
long tapered fingers
finished off in
rose colored polish.
Her beautician
always raved
about her hands
while I hid mine
in my pockets.

And years before,
those same hands
dusted in flour,
kneading, crimping pie crust,
peeling fruit so fast
the knife flowed through apples
slicing the boundary of skin
into strips curling red and white
against the Hoosier cabinet.

The deft hands would pick the peel up,
give it a quick twist,
and pinch the unlike ends together,
red to white,

white to red.
She would laugh and show us
the conundrum
of outside being inside,
inside, outside.
They all spun together —
white hands, red nails,
red outsides, white insides,
but somehow all one surface.

Hands cool on hot foreheads,
gentle on chicken pox,
persistent in pushing needle
through layers of white lawn
meant for a child's naming dress.
Beautiful hands, loving hands,
but still they were hands
that could leave a slap
on her children's pale cheeks;
forever inside and outside,
five fingers
printed in red.

MY MOTHER SAYS —

When baby sleeps, you sleep too.
She's only an infant for ninety days,
might as well sit and hold her,
pass her around the table
to all the neighborhood ladies.
Make some coffee, she says, *but don't*
spill it on the baby.

Roll the tops of your stockings down
and put a knot in them — that way
you don't have to wear a garter belt.
And before you put them on,
rub some mosquito bite cream
into the varicose veins in your ankles.
It's time to go home when your earrings hurt.
And when your feet are cold,
wear socks to bed —

even if you don't wear anything else.

And that, I say,
brings us back to the baby.

WHEN THE DARKTIME COMES

It's like this, dear, my mother says,
her voice coming from far away
like the whispering of old bees in dry clover,
it's like this in the end —
your mother and your best friend,
your sister and your lover
always move away or die,
or they hurt your feelings, and you deny
they ever owned your heart.
Deep inside you can grieve
until you're ready to let sorrow leave
on slow and sticky feet, find a fresh love,
bind yourself to some new Ruth.
In good time and if you're wise,
you'll let these specters rise,
talk good times, and speak old truth.

And that's not all, her voice walks
up my back and cracks
against my word-soaked being,
your children grow up and seeing
you are not the parent of their dreams,
they will hate you until it seems
you must hate them back.
They will judge you and find you wanting;
you will judge them and be haunted
by what you couldn't ever be, couldn't even see
when they were babies
clutching at your skin. Maybe,
if you're lucky, dear, they'll forgive you.
They'll be your friends;

and when the darktimes come,
they'll hold your hands.

The voice is my mother's
but behind her I hear
my grandmother and all the others
before, a shimmer of echoes reaching near
to the gates of the Garden.
Oh children, I ask your pardon.
When the darktimes come, will you hold my hand?
When the darktime comes,
            will you hold my hand?

TWO VIOLINS

It will take two violins
to play the song
that is in my heart
right now.

One, playing pizzicato,
high notes saying,
I am happy for you, my daughter,
flying over the ocean
to the land of our ancestors.

The other is playing
sonorously and so slow,
a sad song,
because you are going
so far away.

I am afraid
you will grow beyond me.
You will find a new mother,
one kinder
and more understanding.

Together, though,
the two violins in my heart
sing a comfort song,
that says, *enough, enough.*
You have worried enough.

OUT OF SEASON

Look into her eyes
and see the tracery of blood,
the child that couldn't be,
the zero instead of the egg,
the part of herself
tumbled into the earth or sea.

First there are those
whose blood is forever waiting,
swept away month after month,
leaving them always hoping,
relieved, perhaps, or resigned —
the ones with no season.

For some the always baby
is named, dressed, and lying
in its closed cradle
rocking with the earth.
These are the lucky ones
for whom the season
was almost right —
they can carry flowers,
talk blood, share guilt.

Then there are the winter ones,
those whose nubby fruit
is wrenched out of season
from their bodies, flushed away
by complicit mother or sister,
gone down the outhouse
while the men are at work,
or, maybe, taken by some masked man

and sent to the sea twelve miles out.
See with what pain
they carry empty jars,
hide blood in dry tears,
keep quiet in crowds.

Spring is the worst season,
when earth purrs and nurses,
and late at night in the back yard
the sharp burn of spent blood
pools unseen in the cold air.

STABAT MATER DOLOROSA

"Stood the mother, full of grief"
13 C. hymn, Jacobus de Benedicta

I.

I am standing here waiting, in joy,
for you to say your first word,
take your first step, defy me
with hands held behind your back,
stamping **no** with your feet,
trying to tear away from my hands
which will not let you go.

And yet you never openly defy me,
just in ways that break my heart.
Telling me you don't care —
how can I comfort you if you don't care?
And the almost lost love —
how can I console you if you won't weep?

II.

The woman who gave me birth
carried me for nine uncomfortable months,
tore herself in two, not for me, but for nature.
My mother was not a cuddler
and this fourth child in six years
got cared for in corners of her days.
But I loved my mother,
her laughter, her games, her stories.

She dressed me in overalls instead of dresses,
let me roam streets, fields and woods.
When my aunt said: *You are ruining that child,*
letting her run wild that way,

my mother whirled on her and said,
Leave her be, she'll do what we never dared,
think what we can't even frame.
She'll find her own way.

III

A few weeks ago I was telling a new doctor
about the almost third baby, miscarried
at five and a half months. She clasped my hands,
cried, *Oh, I'm sorry! It must have been*
very hard for you. I started to say that didn't matter,
but instead I found myself weeping
at the memory of those perfect little hands.

My mother-in-law said I shouldn't
talk about it, certainly not cry.
There will be another one soon enough, she said.
And I never asked about the almost baby,
what happened to it. There was no ceremony
to mark his passing, except this poem.
I never cried and soon there were three more babies,
but there is yet an empty place in my heart
that cries out to feel those shadow hands
                at my breast.

IV

And now dearest of daughters,
you prepare for a child of your own.
The calendar, sonogram, crib, stroller
have an inexorability of their own.
What pleasure at the fluttering
under your heart, what fear
that the little hands and feet will stop,
or never even grow. What joy

comes when the birth is finally over,
the struggling mite is here
looking with eyes that do not see
the long journey from inside to out.

Grief comes with the life
which has not come to pass,
with the remembrance of death,
all the grandmothers, grandfathers
parents, babies — gone into the earth.
I weep for your pain; but you must use it
to cleanse your heart, to love again.
But I know this:
birth always climbs over death,
              a new vine blooming.

coda

Today I read this poem to my husband.
He is shocked at the depth of his not knowing
and says we should, finally, name the little fellow,
so we do: *David Thomas   April 19, 1956.*

IN A DREAM

last night it suddenly came to me:
I must grow up.
I cannot just love, miss the mother,
dead these ten years or more.
I cannot be that little girl,
baby of the family.
I must be the woman who draws
words from pain, caves, canals,
flowings of blood,
who seizes time away
from the young, the beloved.
Let them make their own time,
their own words, free of me
who has fed their bodies,
taken their lives for her own.

I must be the Psyche who smashes
her sisters in their bridal gowns
upon the innocent rocks;
I must be Aphrodite who protects
the Eros within me,
the Naomi who shouts her anger
to the women of Bethelem.

I must be the grown-up,
            mother of myself.

THE WATCH WOMAN POEMS

"Sometimes I jump from memory to memory
as if I were running/ along stones in a stream,"
                              Susan Mitchell

I. Moon Death

Long ago I was
Night Watcher,
Night Woman,
Watch Woman.

In caves cold as winter stars
I was the old grandmother,
wrinkled in tattered dogskins
that left my blue legs and thin arms
open to the bitter air.

At night when the others
entered that little moon death,
I fed the fire piece by piece
to keep them alive,
the men laid out flat,
their mouth-noises shaking the walls,
the women curled on their sides,
their half-grown pups fanned around them,
babies sucking their breasts.

I did this thousands of nights,
always fearful I would let the fire die,
or miss the thawing snakes
crawling in dreadful whispers
from deep inside the mountain
looking for warm blood

ready to flow
over fire-touched stone.

II. Visiting

It is in my blood to keep my eyes open
when the earth turns its dark face
to the stars, so at night,
while daughter and her children sleep,
I slip back into my clothes,
let myself out her back door,
and pad quietly into the shadows
by the wood and wire hutch.
The rabbit sniffs my fingers;
I scratch his solemn nose
and quietly go down the sidewalk
looking for what?
the dark form, perhaps,
of the battering husband,
the dangerous father?
his long, grey car parked
away from the street lights?

I skirt the glimmering puddles
and come to the back gate.
Way down the alley
I think I see red tail-lights,
I think I hear a car
snarling into the empty street,
but there is nothing there now.
I tiptoe back into the house
and, grim as a police station,
settle down with a dull book
until I hear my daughter's footsteps

breaking through the lifting shadows.
This is the signal, the change of guard,
and I can allow myself to sink into sleep,
hearing the children's voices,
happy, or whiny, but safe.

Months later
and a thousand miles away,
I do not even know
when they find the empty hutch
lying open on its side,
the door broken,
a scrap of brown fluff
flung over the fence
its head twisted,
a trickle of blood
on the frozen ground.

III. First Blood

Some of us don't remember this,
but long ago
in old houses
with hallways dark as caves,
in rooms next to sleeping mothers,
we used to wait
for the faintest dry slither
on the oak floor,
a wet hand touching
the white doorknob,
a strange body sliding
through the door,
an invisible mouth whispering
in the stifling darkness.

That's what we do not want to remember —
our unspoken *come here and love me,*
when we should have answered,
stay away or I'll tell Mommy.

It's the dark secret
spreading upward
like shark-drawn blood,
staining everything we think or do,
keeping us hating ourselves
and walking all those hours
until dawn squared the windows
and we have survived one more night.
It is hiding those bad children
nobody could love if they knew,
that makes us shuffle
through houses and streets
when normal people sleep.
It is our first blood
we shed in the dark
that has chilled our lives
all these long and sour years.

IV. Birdsong

At night
I slide carefully out of bed;
in robe and slippers
I wander this old house,
opening doors, turning on lights,
looking in closets.
In winter I sit by the fireplace
tending one last hissing log;
in summer I seek the porch,

my swollen eyes burning,
watching the tiny sparks of life
flaring over the moon-white grass.

There are no children here,
no one who needs my watching,
but still night after night
I sit and rock my body back and forth,
biting my nails until I taste blood,
knowing that in spite of all my care,
I missed the silent coils in the dark,
the diamond head, the hollow fangs
set backwards.

I can only wait
until first birdsong brings
some small redemption,
some forgiveness that comes
with the gift of sun
and sleep.

ALL SAINTS DAY

They walked her from the pond,
her skirts leaving a trail of water
like a car air conditioner, her footsteps outlined
in a phantom track of drying footprints.
Of course she floated —
living on the river that way,
I taught her to ride water
before she could tumble in and drown.
Now her skill has condemned her.

They have set the traffic light
at four-way red
and put up two poles,
one east, one west.
I am tied to the west one,
smashed boxes piled waist high around me.
They tie her to the east one,
place the broken slats around her carefully,
like a Boy Scout campfire.
It is no use crying, begging.
We hold each other's eyes
in fear, in defiance, in love.

First the preacher takes the portable mike
and prays we will be forgiven our blasphemy.
He is serious; he means what he is saying.
He has not slept for days.
I feel sorry for him. He is young.

Next the doctor in his red-striped tie comes
and says how dangerous we could be;
women, he says, whose minds are crazed

like ancient pottery.
He lies and I know why.

Next the bald mayor speaks
about the difficulty of decision,
how he and the council have suffered,
how the town must go on as it always has
The sweat rolls down his face. He suffers.

Then a lady comes pushing a stroller,
the one you always see on TV
screaming at yellow school buses
or women's clinics.
She takes a grill lighter
from the back of the stroller
and snap, snaps it all over
the gas-soaked wood.
Her baby, a stolid boy
in a brown jump suit,
watches a dozen, two dozen
spots of smoke start to curl up.
He reaches his dimpled hand
toward the infant clouds.
I am sorry for him. Such a mother.
The lady pulls her stroller, her baby,
and her lighter back into the crowd,
leaving me colder
than the water I have come from.

Surely they will not make me watch?
The flames run from slat to slat
and the pondwater steams
from her clothes and hair
until suddenly her hair bursts

into a thousand falling stars.
Long after the moaning stops,
she burns like a child's marshmallow
she burns like a dinner candle
  like a birthday candle
  like a wooden match
   going out.
My daughter burns
  until there is nothing left.

They come then and move the boxes away,
untie me,
give me a push
  to start me walking.
I cannot see.

My eyelids seared open,
I stumble everywhere
telling this story,
my one and only story, my daughter.

ARBOR DAY

Today I planted a tree for you.
I dug the hole deep
and hit an old tire graveyard,
but it was enough,
and I slid the little maple in,
tucked up the roots like babies sleeping,
gave it a gallon of surrogate tears,
and then I filled the loose dirt border
with daffodil bulbs — next Spring's yellow stars.

When you needed this
I was too young and hurting
to see
you were too old and hurting
to ask me for it.

This tree will grow as I diminish,
bend down with age.
It will be my private penance
to watch it glow each May
and see you, old dear one,
who squeezed my heart
like a wet dish towel
and hung it out to dry
on the back porch railing.
Too late you wanted to use it
and found it very nearly blown away
on a raucous wind,
hooked on the rose thorns,
almost, but not quite,
                out of your reach.

RAPUNZEL

Rapunzel has let down her long hair
and is gone from the tower.
Oh, lying around the house
are bits of her incipient trades
of student and woman,
and her old trade of daughter —
a half-packed trunk gaping open
beside her white bunk, Chaucer
in Middle English ruffle-paged
across the turtle neck shirts,
her knitting (a tiny swansdown sweater,
half-armed and slightly coffee stained
from where father tripped over the new cat
and slopped his cup) lies yellow
across the blue-checked kitchen cloth,
waiting for her to finish it
for brother's newest; and in the hall
one antique greyed sneaker, frayed
at the outside toe, leans against
the oak wash stand, while its mate
stands upright on the Chinese blue rug
beside last Sunday's comics —
Hagar, to be specific,
or, really, Helga.
All this, and her sleeping form
prone in bed half the daylight hours
but she is really gone already,
released from the tower
by her curly-headed prince,
and still believing in
happily-ever-after-all-things-possible,

while, I, the old witch-mother,
stand here letting her go,
my mouth full
of unspoken words.

VOICES FROM THE LONGEST NIGHT

I.

At the deli counter I take a number,
a low one, for the hour is early
and the crush has not yet started.
The stainless steel pans gleam and wink
in the faint flicker of the florescent tubes,
each rectangle framing a gorgeous mound
of salad: three kinds of macaroni, four of potato,
three slaws, various arrays of succulent fruits.
My mouth waters at the chicken and turkey,
at the cheeses in all their colors of captured light.
The breads, long, thin and golden, or round and dark,
are stacked ready for destruction.

Mama, I am so hungry, Mama.

I hand the elderly man my square of plastic
and notice the blue numbers permanently inked
up his forearm, the tell-tale crossed sevens
standing out like Calvary.
Frozen back in time, I stare at him,
but actually I am looking inward at an old magazine
    picture
of a naked baby, two years old, perhaps,
every bone visible through his tight skin,
the shadows under his blue eyes so dark
they dominate his face. They are his face.

Mama, I am so cold. Mama where are you?

And I hear a soldier's voice telling about
the liberation of a death camp:

I opened a door,
and I thought it was cordwood
stacked so neatly against the weather,
but when my sergeant brought the light,
it was babies, arms and legs like twigs,
dead babies stacked to the ceiling
waiting for room in the furnace.

They never leave my dreams. If only they would cry,
I'd know I could do something.

In my sudden dumbness my throat
is locked tight with long-borne guilt.
I know if I try to speak I will cry.
The deli man flushes, pales, and says:

The roast beef is good today, Mrs.
You want that?

I nod and watch his flashing knife decapitate the bread,
slice savagely through the rosy meat,
lay the tomatoes open like fresh, red wounds.
His hands so swift I almost cannot follow them,
he layers the slices compactly,
slaps a spoonful of pale mustard on top,
reaches me the sandwich on a paper plate.

Papa, I am so hungry, Papa.

Noticing the numbers that way, I have offended him,
intruded on something I can never share.
His children starved, perhaps, evaporated into flame,
while I crouched safely
in the basement of an American school,
my head bent between my knees,

dreading the bombers that never did come.
What could I ever know of his suffering?

Papa, papa, come back. Don't leave me! Don't leave me.

The next day when I come to the deli
he is wearing a long sleeved shirt.
Mrs. I beg you — leave me alone.

II.
At the table where I take my lunch
someone has left a newspaper.
Three blonde women, each with the air of a Mona Lisa,
gaze serenely from the front page.
Even the smudgy grays of newsprint
cannot hide their beauty,
the slanted slavic eyes like foxes',
the cheekbone lines that spell
sister, sister, sister.
But that is not what holds me —
it is the eyes deep with old sorrow, old pain
belying the joyful smiles.

The headline shouts:

**BURIED ALIVE, SISTERS
SURVIVE HOLOCAUST, MEET SAVIORS
FORTY YEARS AFTER**

*Why me? Why me? To save me
they sentenced me living to the tomb,
not to Hell by fire, but Hell by cold,
Hell by hunger, Hell — by silence.*

Polish Jews, the sisters wait in the airport

for their Christian saviors, an elderly farm couple
stumbling along the pleated ramp,
disoriented by time and lights and jet engines,
bewildered at the necessity for this reunion
so long after the buried sisters, children then,
arose from the trench under the farmhouse floor
and fled with the six adult living corpses
into an April resurrection,
finally safe from the Nazi soldiers
swilling and stamping overhead.
The sisters remember their parents begging the couple
to put poison in the jugs of milk and soup they pass down
into the grave every night after the household sleeps,
but, no, the Polish farmer says:

We all live, together,
or we all die, together.
There is no way in-between.

III.

Shamans, prophets and seers know
the importance of entering another's dream,
for only truth is told in such sacred world.

That night in my dreams
I am a cold Jew, a cold, cold Jew;
I am a sandwich of Jews,
all of us turning together in the dark.

I am Sarah, a small girl child
growing horizontally in the dark earth
knowing only the demands of the human body,
the torments of confinement,
the dread silence of the tomb.
Our parents can tell us nothing,

teach us nothing, cannot risk some
night wanderer, some Aryan Grendel
hearing our Yiddish whispers.

I crust with dirt and excrement;
my sharp bones burst through my nursery clothes;
my nails grow long and curled like badger claws;
my baby teeth fall out and disappear.
Slowly my eyes seal shut;
why should I open them
when there is nothing to see
but darkness and deeper darkness?

Two and a half years my sisters and I sleep under the
earth.
I do not talk or cry or laugh for I have never lived.
I do not know that outside on the shortest sunlit day
brown sparrows twitter in green pines;
and on the longest night white foxes
unpack themselves from their litter mates,
slip out of their dens into starlight,
tunnel black noses into the snow,
toss it high in the sharp air,
leap after it, joyously barking,
forelegs spread, hind legs in point,
bushy tails dancing, dancing
under the solstice moon.

Shadow foxes.

Wounded earth.

Buried children
sleeping
through the longest night.

THE WEB

You know how it is with an April day...
                              Robert Frost

Once on Spring break I visited my daughter
for a whole week and we stepped around icy puddles
and slogged through muddy ruts
reciting *Two Tramps in Mud Time*, almost
falling over in our joy at seeing each other.
Arms entwined we made a pilgrimage
to an inner library cavern where some Janizary
did not come and clean out the poet's books,
his old grey sweater, and his Morris chair
which had made two trips across the ocean
to keep the poet company and to provide
arms to rest a board on for when he wrote
longhand on sheets of yellow paper — poems.
My daughter said she had a friend who late at night
would pull the sweater on, sit in the chair
and pretend to be busy at the writing board.
Then they would laugh uproariously
at the thought how shocked all the ladies
who "did" poetry would be if they saw him.

And we drove up his farm lane in Ripton,
evoking my mother in a ritual of remembering the stag
she had told us about who came out of the woods
one warm October day and stood looking at her
with dark eyes for a long moment.
Suddenly she noticed a truck creeping up behind them.
She leaned on the horn and the deer was gone in a flash.
The hunters in the truck cursed her, but
she only said gently, "I'm sorry; I didn't notice you."

It was one the best lies she ever told, she said later.
Then one cold day we headed over the mountain
on miles of corduroy roads still drifted in snow
to visit the ghost of my grandmother,
to imagine all four feet nine of her
living in the little granite house
with the cherry thresholds that
her first husband built for her,
while she, at seventeen,
was having her first baby.

The sun was warm but the wind was chill...

Then we went back up the hill to the house
her second husband built for her,
a much richer place with white clapboard
and great bay windows looking down the valley.
He wasn't a quarryman like the first one;
        he owned the quarry,
and some said he had taken steps to see
that my grandfather could run from the big hook
on the derrick, but couldn't escape it.
My grandfather took three days to die
leaving a widow only twenty-five years old.

We took the long way home, down the valley,
and through a woods so dark and deep
we almost missed the sign that indicated
another poet lived there,
        providentially named *Stone*.
On we went and circled back to the place
we started from, marble dormitory steps,
where we hugged and kissed good-bye,
completing the web, the story, the moving line.

HAWK AT THE BRIDGE

As one does in dreams,
I am suddenly transposed
to a room by the bridge
in Lambertville, New Jersey,
a room where I look out
a large window at a cage
dangling on a white-trimmed porch.
Look, an owl, I say,
and I go out for a closer look.

It isn't an owl,
but a hawk half in
and half out of the cage.
With my hands I deliver her
through the cage door.
She nestles her wild self
in my arms for a moment,
holding her iron claws delicately curled.
Then she takes off out the window
        and into the wind
far over the river and bridge.

I recognize that shining head,
that proud sweep of wing —
        it is my daughter I have freed.

MY MOTHER'S HANDS

My grownup daughter asks me;
astonishment in her voice,
When did you get grandma's hands?

I didn't answer her,
but I wanted to —
somewhere in the thousands
   of apple peelings
   tomato skins
   bread and butter pickles
   dripping noses
   swimming lessons
   laundry done on a scrub board
   diapers washed
   baby bottoms tended

somewhere in all that mess,
your hands
         will become like mine.

SLEEPING BEAUTY, AWAKENING

You touched me
and a warm wind, a south wind,
blew over my heart
melting the blue glacier
that crept along my veins
like some ice-age Goliath
stringing freezing Northway fjords
on crystal bitter cords.

You touched me
and a warm wind, a south wind,
whirled through my mind
freeing a whole ballet
of gold and white butterflies
to pirouette
in giddy gladness
through sudden April madness.

You touched me
and a warm wind, a south wind,
filled my blank soul,
sleeping these hundred years,
with the scent of wild roses
that called forth
this piercing unknown desire
that leaps like magic midnight fire.

You touched me
and some nameless sorcery hovered,
borne on that philtered breeze,
lifted my hand to stroke your cheek
and willed my unfolding voice to speak
in secret words and name you —
                    Beloved.

SOUL MATES

"Lovers don't finally meet somewhere.
They're in each other all along."
                    Rumi

We crawled out of the sea together, you and I,
  two paramecia making microscopic
    footprints in primeval sand.
We raced the plains of the Serengeti
  and chased each other through
    the jungle top, two hairy children
    in the morning of history.
I was there when you took fire
  from the lightning and
    released the vultures of flame
      that ate your own beautiful flesh.
      Ah, Prometheus, how I watched
        and wept over your suffering
          and could not beat away
            the birds of death.
Together we took shelter in the caves from the ice
  and spent eons in the joy of painting
    red and brown deer bounding over the walls.
      Each day I was afraid when you left
        for the hunt. You brought me
          the warmest skins, the largest
            meats, but without you, what
              is skin or meat?
I'm not sorry I got us put out of
  The Garden, Adam. Would you really
    have liked to live as two pretty
      babies for all time? Never to know
        the surging joy of love? the tearing
          pain of sorrow? the delight and

responsibility of creation? the
quiet passion of a growing mind?
Oh, it was beautiful,The Garden,
but it was so flat and dull.
Without the valleys, Adam,
would we ever know the peaks?
Remember, my love, when we sailed the Nile together?
When I was the Beauty of the World and you were
the conqueror of men? And I remember, my Antony,
how you sheltered my body from their whips and stones.
But it was no use. We died, and our children died,
because politics doesn't recognize love.
My darling Abelard, I am still overcome with shame
at the terrible humiliation my flirtation
brought upon you. I told my uncle it was I, Heloise,
who seduced the dark-eyed priest, but he had to
punish you as well, my dear. What losses we
suffered for love — your manhood, our baby,
shut away from the world and apart from each other —
but our letters, Peter Abelard, we left the world
our letters!
Now, Albert, I know I was crabby,
but, my heavens, nine children
and all of England to take care of,
to say nothing of Ireland, it's
no wonder I was a little cranky.
Forget that I nagged you.
Forget that I was jealous.
Just remember —
Victoria loved Albert.

All these years, all these lifetimes —
and still our love is not through.
It will come again when we are gone,
in another form — newly born.

A FINE LIFE

*I wondered whether the life that was right for one was
ever right for two*

Willa Cather

Fifty years we have lived together
and five times our secret dwellers
have met in a warm, red cellar to make a new heart
beating in the tiny rhythm of the burgeoning unborn.
Five times I have gone apart from you
and been torn in two, crying and spilling
my blood for the tree of life, venerating
this arcane force that pushed
the two of us into seven.

Some of our fights have been spectacular
or a spectacle, depending on your point of view,
like the time I threw a summer squash at you.
It spattered on the wall dripping strings of seeds
into the black coffee grounds from the pot I threw too.
You laughed and together we cleaned up the mess.
That weekend, things between us were a little cool.

But to counter-balance, there were places when love
was more than hot, like the bank of day lilies
nodding knowing orange spots over our lovers' knot,
while a voyeuer muskrat stood on his snakey tail,
blinked his eyes, and watched beside our beached
    canoe.
Quieter we breathed until you, laughing,
picked a drooping flower, named it, *screw-weed*.

But sometimes the flower dried, curled up deep inside,

like our love that winter night we sat house-weary on the stairs
each rocking a diapered burden and dreaming of our own
    affairs —
yours with numbers you follow till you catch and hold them
in your eye, fill the hollow in your mind with Lorelei;
mine with wracking words so wild I cannot help but wallow
naked in bound sheets of shrieking, damned poets,

Yes, fifty years we have lived together
and our children have vanished into their own fine lives.
I still open at night to your rising,
listen to your dreams. My love,
you bring me coffee in bed;
Saturdays you say, *What'll we do today?*

SOUL TRAPPERS

We trapped you, didn't we?
At some moment in the primal embrace
we called in the bits and fragments of baby souls
tumbling out there in the void,
(or did you, as the Indians say,
fly up my dress when I walked over
infant bones buried in the forest path?)

Once you were settled in,
comfortable in the red nest,
you gave the pattern,
I made the cases,
little fat sausages with matchstick arms,
pencil legs, and big wobbly heads.
(Already you carried the restless seeds
that would fill more red nests to bursting.)

You were all so different —
wolves and rabbits,
squirrels, foxes and singing birds.
We almost drowned in your needs,
your resistance to being human.
When you left the connectors stretched,
thinned, but never broke;
when you found your other selves,
filled your nests,
our world widened to take them in.

In the end, I think you trapped us
as much as we trapped you.
You took us along
into a giant kaleidoscope

of red and blue,
green and yellow,
even white and black,
our senses shifting with the light,
and all woven together
in love and pain
love and joy
love.

AT THE Y

It is the turning of the year
when anything you might imagine
can happen among the swirling leaves
all gone yellow and red and lacey.
But it happens at the Y, yes I see them!

The Venus of Willendorf,
with her splendid hips,
round haunches,
and stomach sagging
from too many babies,
sitting on a bench
in the ladies' dressing room.

And Isis stepping out of the shower
like she was born out of a blossom,
dainty high-arched feet, legs long
and tapered springing from chalice of hips.
Breasts as perfect as peaches,
long, dark, wet hair framing,
yes, a dark-eyed, lovely face.

She smiles at me.
She knows how beautiful she is.

BABY STEPS

In the space between one night and another
I am thrust back into my childhood,
my babyhood, even. I was surprised
this could happen to me; not scared,
surprised — and angry.

At first I could not walk or talk.
Waking up in the hospital like that,
I was embarrassed I was there.
I pretended every thing was just fine,
and I was holding court
from my high bed
just as my mother used to,
nodding my head a little
to say it was all right.

At first I could not swallow
so the food was ground up for me.
I didn't like it, and not being able
to reach for the spoon
with my hand this way,
I spilled most of it on my clothes.
I had to wear a bib
just like my baby granddaughter.

She, the baby, takes great pleasure in walking
with her one hand held tightly in her mother's.
I finally walk too, my hand
grasped around of the head of my cane,
or my husband carefully steering
my elbow to places
I would no longer to dare to go.

The time is all full of first days:
when I go to the bathroom I forget
the tubes fastened to my arm
and they are firmly shut in the door.
The nurse gasps to see what I have done.
When she straightens me all out
I say, *Thank you*, like a good girl should,
and these are my first words.

THE DRESSER POEMS

I. The Chapel

Noble Dog lies across the threshold
seeking to tangle my hesitating feet in his tail or paws
and thus throw me into the space
that I have come to think of as my chapel.

Lying here all these months after my stroke,
I see the holiness of this room,
with its 8 over 8 window panes
looking out on a tiny woodland
grown up on the embankment. In summertime
the leaves are so thick and green
I cannot see the trains on top of the berm,
only hear them, their heaviness so great
I sense them from a long way away.
By day I see the great and lovely trumpets
from the Rose of Sharon shouting
I will not die, I will not die,
            but they do.
They last well into September
and finally give way to the mauve
and russet leaves that mean the turning
of the year approaches.
The excursion trains come then,
with their whistling at Toad Lane,
the *hoo-hoo-oo-hoo* of the steam engine,
or a Great Barred owl, *Pallas Athena,*
calling me to resist the bearing down,
to fly over the silver rails in steady wingbeats.
Is it the owl — or *Minerva* — or me?

Then *Demeter and Persephone* really get down to work,
stripping the curling leaves from their branches,
throwing sleet, hail, and snowballs at each other,
until we are deep into winter.
Water seeps through the panes
covering them with thick-ribbed ice,
until I am forced back into the white walls
of my igloo, or kiva, or Mary Chapel.
Around the top of the room
there is a blue border of eyelet
that matches the eyelet skirt on the bed,
the dais that only one God has ever come to.
A blue and white wedding ring quilt
and a blue and gray rag rug on the floor
satisfy my need for blue and for circles.
But there are three more I take to my heart —
high over the bed there is a big oil of the Hudson River,
blue, blue, *Lorelei* singing from the moonlit water:
Ich weiss nicht was soll es bedeuten,
    dass ich so traurig bin,
an acrylic print of the world, *Gaea, Tiamat, Nut,*
a glorious swirl of blue and white, green and yellow.
Then there is *Moon Bridge*, an intaglio print
meant, I am sure, for *Inanna* the Moon Goddess.
There are circles within circles, moon reflecting moon,
arches reflecting arches, people on the bridge
with their backs to the reality,
watching the moon in the water,
all set an in an egg-shaped oval.

The sun is again spilling through the windows,
the magpie, prophetic bird, tells us

there is death in life, life in death.
Spring is pushing blue flowers through the myrtle —

worshipping Aphrodite.

II. The Rosary

Hail Mary, Full of Grace,
pray for us sinners
now and at the hour of our need. Amen.

My shoulder has stiffened until it cannot move;
my daughter-in-law says my arm will wither away
if I don't do something about it,
but high priestesses of therapy
provoke it into mobility again.
This is how they do it: they alternately
put moist heat and ice on my shoulder
and they tie my hand behind my back
    with a rubber bandage
until the pain is excruciating — then they leave it that way
for twenty minutes. I do not make a sound,
but I am ready to throw up.
She comes just in time and unties me, forces my arm forward
until it snaps audibly.

There is no gain without pain, she says cheerfully,
and that becomes the watchword of my recovery.
Relax, relax, she murmurs, and rubs my arm in a certain way,
teasing the muscles out of their tension.
Let it sink into the pain and come out the other side, she says.

Hail Mary

Every morning I go through the same routine:
I take a pad of moist heat

and tie it laboriously around my neck
using just my left hand to make a bow knot.
(I am justly proud of this accomplishment.)
Lying flat on my back and holding a can of cherries
(it is just the right weight), I allow it to push my arm down
over my head, and I hold it for twenty minutes —
then the other the way. I will my flesh
to relax into the cleansing pain.
I am sweating when it is done,
but there still is more to do with these damn cherries.
I lift the can over my head and to the side,
up and down, back and forth for thirty times,
thirty shekels, 3 x 10 — the magic number is three,
as it always has been —
and somewhere in the last ten motions
the pain, slinking away, disappears.   *Amen.*

Then comes the ice bag — fire and ice
so says Revelations, and the ice washes away
all the pain for another twenty minutes
while I read poetry out loud
      to control my stumbling tongue,
to bring it to the fire and make it jump through.
I have been at this for more than an hour now,

and still we are not done.

Hail Mary

There are the cane exercises, three cans of soup
wrapped around the cane with a strap
which I lift up in four ways
for thirty times — 120 three pound lifts.
I wrap the rubber band around my wrist

and make inward and outward pulls
for another thirty times.
Then there is the pulley suspended from a hook
with a rope and two handles. The hardest of all,
my back to the wall
and my hand bent behind my back
being pulled back and forth, up and down
in one swing of the pulley. Twice thirty times.

Then it is finished. No more pain.

It is the Mass, the moment of transubstantiation,
the moment when mind takes the place of muscle.

Ete missae est.

Amen

III. The Dresser

> *Until the day break, and the shadows flee away.*
> *Jane Amelia   August 4th, 1908*
> Union Cemetery Tombstone

With my back to wall
I can see the lonely snow robin
grasping a grey branch on a grey day,
only her pumpkin breast
saving the picture from sadness.

Sarasvati

Her beak points the way to the dresser,
a hundred fifty years old,
made before the Civil War.
It was in the attic of the last house we bought,

and the old man we got it from said:
You want it? My girls don't care anything about it —
and the limoge-es tea cups — you can have them.
I could hardly believe my luck, and on my birthday too.

It had belonged to Arthur's grandmother
and then his mother, both named Mary.
His grandfather had bought a pair of bureaus
and a wooden rocker to rock babies in,
along about 1856. Arthur's second wife had sent them
to the attic just a hundred years later, but
Arthur gave one of the dressers to the Methodist Church.
They painted it white.

Cybele

After the dark finish was off the first dresser
it was truly a beautiful thing —
a nice tight grain scrolled across
light tulip wood, four dark petals carved
around a center, repeated
on each of three drawers,
and brass drawer pulls shined
until they were sunlight across the golden wood.

I never could get the Methodist one back,
offered them money and everything.
I imagine it still up in the attic over the manse.
The dresser has been mine for over forty years
and still I wonder about that first Mary,
how she stirs my clothes, makes my scarves
and nightgowns breathe.

IV. Over the Dresser

> *She should be the visible moon: impartial, loving,*
> *severe, wise.* Robert Graves *The White Goddess*

My daughters would like to have the mirror
over the dresser, but I think not for a little while longer.

My grandmother painted roses on it
and gave it to me for my fourth birthday
in 1936, the year we sat in the rocker together
and broke it. My mother was not pleased,
not with me, not with her.

It wasn't the broken chair she minded;
it was the loss of control over me
and my grandmother that got her gall up.

Waiting for my brother to come home
from the five & ten downtown,
with a package of clay for me
I wet my pants, ski pants at that.
Then I yelled at my mother that it was her fault
since she had fastened the safety pin
to my shoulder where I couldn't reach it.

You could have done better than that,
she said grimly. I answered,
so could you,
and that's when
she got really mad.

It wasn't the spanking I minded;
it was being put to bed without my supper,
and the brightness I was missing

of everybody being home
at the same time — my sister and brothers,
my mother and father, and particularly
the mother of my father
who had never shown up before this winter,
and would never show up again in my lifetime.

My grandmother, as wide as she was tall,
sneaked up the back stairway
with some mashed potatoes and gravy for me.
And after that we went into the little attic room
over the log cabin of the house
where one of my grandmother's rockers
was waiting for us to sit down and rock.
She read to me: *Baucis* and *Philemon,*
how their love for each other
turned them into a twining linden and oak
growing from the same trunk,
Atalanta and the race for the Golden Apples,
Iphigenia and *Orestes* and their wonderful escape — .
I was just about asleep
when the rocker rocked its last
and with a mighty *crash*
sent us sprawling on the cold and splintery floor.

Everyone raced upstairs from the dining room,
my mother making her ponderous way
to the final judgment,
which I didn't hear because this time
I really was put to bed.

The next morning my grandmother was gone,
back to her home in Vermont.
When my birthday rolled around

my mother said to me, *well, here's this mirror —*
you can put it up over the dresser.

V. On the Dresser

lies a fine linen scarf
my mother-in-law made for me,
cross-stitching it with delicate roses
to match the mirror, and in the center
is a natural birch jewelry box
my middle son made long ago in shop class,
mitering its drawers so carefully
and finishing it to a soft gleam.
It is where I keep jewelry I would never wear,
and funeral cards of people I have loved.
In front of the box there is a basket in which
I throw the crosses and hearts and earrings
I have just taken off — where they lie
in a tangle of gold and silver icons.
The cross keeps me mindful of my youngest son
who tells the story over and over again
of God's ritual suffering.

Gaea, Macha, Hathor, Rhea

To the right is our bridal picture,
softly colored, as they used to do,
my mitts and collar embroidered to match my veil,
my dress fashioned from a cloud.
My Honey looks out from under
his rich dark curls with eyes as black as a witch's.
We are beautiful.

Eos, Sedna, Cybele, Usha

Stuck in the mirror frame is a picture of my mother
the last time she visited us.
She is too weak to get off the brown couch.
After her leaving — well, I wasn't done with her yet.
And there's another snapshot too — all five of the children
surrounding the youngest daughter's bridegroom,
all of them looking so happy on her wedding day.

Isis, Hera, Aphrodite, Frija

In front of the picture is a flock of snow sparrows
which I love for no particular reason —
I bought them myself at a dollar apiece.
Close by the little birds is a smooth,
egg-shaped rock with a sign from the Zodiac
painted on it in black — Gemini, two faces
turned to each other. My eldest daughter made it
years ago for a May birthday gift.
I like the feel of it, its smoothness,
and the fact that she gave it to me
when she had nothing else to give.

Sarasvati, Jahi, Ishtar

On the right side of the dresser there is a lamp,
a fake Victorian hurricane lamp
    with globes that do not match
since I broke the top one
and found another looking like an ivory moon.
I like it just the way it is.
Next is a small wooden box
with a tile set into its cover
and on the tile there is a brown beaver
carrying a stick through the water

just as we had observed one evening
when we were walking along the canal.
We watched him every night for weeks
praying no one else would notice him,
but one day the ranger caught him in a trap
and transported him far up the Delaware.
And finally there is a tiny hollowed-out black cat
with flowers painted all over it
which I keep my Christmas earrings in —
a pair my eldest son gave me so long ago
he does not remember the giving, but I do.
Inanna, Hecate, Nokomis, Danu

This dresser is where earth and moon goddesses
come to comfort me and be comforted.

Gaea, Danu, Macha, Rhea, Hathor (the cow goddess),
Nokomis, Juno, Cybele (the goddess of caves)
Sarasvati, Sedna, Ishtar (the wild one),
Hecate, Selene, Jahi (the bringer of moon blood)
Isis, Mary, Hera, Frija (the giver of children),
and don't forget Oduduwa, (the womb of the world),
Spider Woman, Bast with the head of a cat,
    and Eos or Ushas
(daughter of time, bearer of winds, bringer of dawn).

IN MY DREAMTIME

The dead have their work to do.   Rilke

My sister continues to grow in my dreams
from the forever girl she once was
   to a vibrant young woman
like my daughters.
   She has a mass of brown hair
touched with red and gold;
   her voice has changed
from a low inchoate mumble
   to happy sparkling words.

I am sorry for all the times
   I took advantage of her –
   borrowing her skirts and blouses,
   and, once, a pair of platform shoes,
high heeled, gold studs around the sole.
   I broke the heel on one,
answered her unasked question:
   I was dancing, I was dancing.

She knew I was lying.

She came again last night.
   She is living far to the north
in a cabin with chinked logs.
   Her two little girls, Ariel and Rosie,
are carbon copies of my sister.
   Rosie has just tinkled on the doorstep.
That's when it begins to get confusing.
   At first she calls me *Aunt Pat*, then
she says, *Grandma won't spank you,*
   as if I ever would —.

In my dreamtime I have become
   my sister's mother.

WASHING THE FEET OF THE PROPHET

(a lament for Martha Bernays Freud)

He stripped me naked with his dark eyes
and I could never resist for long.
He always won and I had to give up
my pals, my boy cousins.
Dear little girl, he said,
you don't need them — only me.
I will teach you everything
you will ever need to know.
Scarce two days after our wedding,
he stayed my hand
from lighting the Sabbath candles,
so God never entered our home.
More things than candlelight
never came to birth that night.

Mourning my God,
I knew right then
he loved someone else more than me,
something else more than life —
it was that little lustful boyself,
that child consumed by desire,
that infant satyr, Joy,
who would never be satisfied,
certainly not by me.
And mourning my God, I watched
while he dipped his fingers in death
every day, loving it,
loving his dead statues and paintings,
dustcatchers all,
loving his foul cigars

dropping ashes on the rugs
and stinking of the grave.
Mourning my God,
I probed my eye-wells for tears
and washed the feet of the prophet
with my greying hair.

All those days
of keeping the children quiet
so his patients and homburgs
wouldn't hear them,
of getting his meat and potatoes
on the table right on time,
and keeping the children quiet
while his friends ate my cooking,
never tasting it as they rumbled on.
And keeping the children quiet
while he wrote his letters
and papers evening after evening.
I lost my voice
keeping the children quiet.

He left me warming the bed alone,
the bed he seldom came to
after little Anna was born.
He could have talked to me —
I wasn't stupid, only quiet in my rage.
Instead, he talked to my sister.
Warming the bed alone,
I seethed at all those rich useless women
who could buy his hours and his mind,
telling him the gossip
they knew he wanted to hear.

All those nights he was away,
and he never thought of taking me.
I finally turned to stone.

During a lifetime
of mourning my God,
keeping the children quiet,
warming the bed alone,
I placed tuning forks in my ears,
anointed my eyes with lamp oil,
wired my jaw to an empty door.
Washing the feet of the prophet —
I tore the flesh right off
my hands and knees,
my blood swirling red as clay
in the white basin,

and he never noticed.

MOTHER TONGUE

I was there when it happened.
They saw me as the useless old crone,
mindless, mute, no threat. The sun
shone through the summer trees when they did it —
took the young women captives
and cut out their tongues.
I saw them — one would pin her arms,
one would grab her hair, hold her head back
so her jaw and mouth jutted forward.
Another pulled her jaw down and wedged
a stick deep in her mouth.
    Then they did it —
sliced through the tongue with their knives,
sometimes the cheeks went too,
skin fluttering like the leaves overhead.
And on the ground —
        tongues leaping
            like little wounded animals.

Silenced, these these women
    would never corrupt their children.
These dams would never turn issue against sire.

    But I saw it, I collected the tongues, picked them up
one by one and dropped them in a soft deerskin bag
where they comforted one another
while I waited for the children to be born,
to grow up speaking only the father's language
until years or centuries later
when I took them secretly to the forest
and gave each daughter, each son

the mother's tongue, grown hard with time,
sharp with the bitter herbs that preserved them.
Now, I said, *you have a weapon*
more powerful than knives.
Keep it burnished, practice with it,
hand it down to your daughters and sons
until one day there will be enough of you
for the ancient spilled blood
to renew itself in a grand language
where words are knives excising lies,
a time when no one can be silenced.

Then I blessed them and said,

> **Go, Children,**
> **and reclaim**
> **your Mother Tongue.**

Acknowledgments

Grateful acknowledgment is made to the editors of the following magazines or
books in which these poems first appeared, perhaps in a slightly different format:

Before the Beginning:	"Dear Little Sister,"
	"Rapunzel"
A Different Latitude:	"When the Darktime Comes"
Dodge Picnic Poems:	"My Mother Says —"
Dodge Poet Chapbook Series:	"Wild Apples"
The Dresser Poems Chapbook:	"Baby Steps"
published for the Elizabeth M. Boggs	"Guardian Angel"
Center for Accessibilities UMDNJ	"The Chapel"
Conference on Accessibilities	"The Rosary"
	"The Dresser"
	"Over the Dresser"
	"On the Dresser"
	"When the Dark Time Comes"
Journal of Accessibilities:	"Out of the Stars"
Mother's Day Chapbook:	"Mother Tongue"
	"Soul Trappers"
The Paterson Review:	"My Mother Says — "
	"The Rosary"
	"The Dresser"
	"Over the Dresser"
	"Sundown Tomorrow"
The River:	"The Dresser"
Stone Country:	"Wild Apples"
Tree House Press:	"The Dresser Poems: After the Stroke"
	"Hoo Doo Doll"
U S 1 Worksheets:	"At the Y"
	"Hawk at the Bridge"

I would also like to gratefully acknowledge HM in the Founder's Award, The
National Federation of State Societies, for "When the Darktime Comes," and
HM in the Allen Ginsberg Award for "Over the Dresser."

About the Author

Patricia Celley Groth taught English, Writing, and Women's
Studies at Rutgers University, The College of New Jersey,
and Shimer College. She is a Dodge poet and has received
two fellowships from The New Jersey Council on the Arts .
She has published over one hundred poems in magazines
and journals; two books, *Before the Beginning,* and *The
Gods' Eyes;* and several articles. She has had three plays
produced, won many prizes, edited three anthologies of
contemporary poetry, and is a member of Delaware Valley
Poets, Inc., U. S. 1, and Beaver Pond Poetry Forum. She is
married, has five children and fourteen grandchildren.

Index